A COLLECTION OF WEEKLY RADIO MESSAGES BY

R.J. RUSHDOONY

GOOD MORNING, FRIENDS

VOLUME 2

EDITED BY SUSAN BURNS

CHALCEDON/ROSS HOUSE BOOKS
VALLECITO, CALIFORNIA

Ross House Books
PO Box 158
Vallecito, CA 95251
www.ChalcedonStore.com

Library of Congress: 2017942694

10 digit: 1-879998-80-7
13 digit: 978-1-879998-80-3

Printed in the United States of America

CONTENTS

CRISES AND GOD

September 14, 1954

Good morning, friends. One of the things which makes life a little harder these days is the newspaper. All one has to do to find something to worry about is to read a newspaper and listen to some news commentator. They give us a fairly steady diet of wars and rumors of war, storms, accidents, murders, scandals, and the like. Try mixing all that into your breakfast, and you've got a good reason for ulcers!

Now, I have no intention of suggesting that you cancel your daily paper. I certainly don't intend to do so. I do suggest, though, that we look at these constantly recurring human tragedies from a healthy perspective.

First of all, we have to recognize that the history of the world is one of perpetual human crises. All recorded history gives us essentially the same story: civilization tottering, man in despair, ugliness of behavior, human depredations and depravity, it's all an old story. As Christians we not only must recognize that this has been so, we must insist that it will be so. The history of the world will be a perpetually recurring crisis because man is in rebellion against God. You cannot take rotten

1

lumber, eaten by termites and dry rot, and build a good house. Neither can you take man the sinner and build a paradise on earth. Man keeps demanding two things, peace and security, and dreams of a trouble-free world with cradle-to-grave security and only creates a hell on earth instead. Forty centuries and more before Christ, men dreamed of a human paradise, a world parliament of nations, and the like. Assyria tried to force a one-world concept on the nations, and only destroyed itself in the process. There is no peace or security apart from God, and every effort to attain them is doomed to frustration. As long as there is a God of justice, there will be the kind of world we see around us. If the world tomorrow gained the kind of peace we hanker for, it would be the greatest act of divine injustice that could be imagined. Man has no peace in his own heart: how can he hope to live in peace with anyone? Man apart from God is a shaking reed, a ferment of insecurity. How can any outward condition give him security? Man himself destroys his peace, and wrecks his own efforts at security. When mankind is not made up of saints and angels, it is no wonder that this world will not be a heaven. Thus history is in a constant recurring state of crises and will continue to be so. This is a fact which we must accept, a grim fact, but a fact of justice.

> **WE ARE MORE READY TO READ ABOUT WAR AND SCANDAL THAN WE ARE TO READ THE BIBLE: WE ENJOY OUR TROUBLES FAR MORE.**

Second, we must recognize that this very condition of

crisis is a part of God's justice and therefore under His control. We all have moments of discouragement when we feel that things are all wrong and hopelessly out of control. We need, then, to turn to the book of Genesis and read the history of Joseph in chapters thirty-seven to fifty. Here we see a growing tragedy: a family divided and corrupt, brothers betraying their father and selling their brother into slavery; the brother suffering injustice as a slave and ending up in prison, forgotten by man and left to rot with none to remember him. Life seems often to deal with us in this manner. We feel like crying out with Jacob, "All these things are against me." But God never forgets: step by step all the evil of man is converted into good by His total providence: Joseph rules over Egypt and sees the blessing in all his suffering. This is the history of God's people: the outcome is certain, although often it is apparent only in eternity. The world is not out of God's control: it is held tightly in His Almighty hands. To us it seems chaos only because we cannot see the pattern that is being woven. But in quiet confidence shall be our strength, and in trusting Him our surest reward.

The crises of which the newspapers write, the horror and tragedy, are in themselves a horror. But nothing in this world exists in itself: all exist against the background and within the orbit of God's providence, and no act is final in itself. When God's reckoning is made, the meaning will be made plain to all.

Third, we must recognize that there is more to our world than the crises we read of. Remember, the life, death, and resurrection of our Lord are the determining factors of all human history, and they are not daily recorded as the basic factor in all news. Remember, too, that your life and mine have been rich in God's providence and blessing: our years have been filled with His goodness. Yet the rare occasions when our lives enter the news is usually when we have an accident or are in trouble. A million people can fly safely, but let ten die, and that alone is news. Every rumor of war is news, but a hundred thousand converts to Christ in Asia is not news. Our very concept of news tells us something about man, about ourselves, that man is looking for trouble, and that we delight in it. We are more ready to read about war and scandal than we are to read the Bible: we enjoy our troubles far more. We are more ready to talk about somebody's sins than to praise his goodness, more ready to gossip than to pray. We all have this weakness.

If we walk more closely with God in Christ, we will have more of His peace and confidence.

He says to us:

They shall not be ashamed that wait for me. (Isa. 49:23).

Said I not unto thee, that if thou wouldest believe, thou shouldest see the glory of God? (John 11:40)

I prayed; and the Lord hath given me my petition which I asked of him. (1 Sam. 1:27)

My heart rejoiceth in the Lord. (1 Sam. 2:1)

Come and hear, all ye that fear God, and I will declare what he hath done for my soul.

Blessed be God, which hath not turned away my prayer, nor his mercy from me. (Ps. 66:16, 20)

When the waves thereof arise, thou stillest them. (Ps. 89:9)

He maketh the storm a calm, so that the waves thereof are still ... so he bringeth them unto their desired haven. Oh that men would praise the Lord for his goodness. (Ps. 107:29–31)

Blessed is the man that trusteth in him. (Ps. 34:8)

FEAR AND PATIENCE

January 3, 1956

Good morning, friends. Fear and flight are commonly associated as cause and effect, and rightly so. When people are afraid, the usual impulse is to run away. But fear often disguises itself as courage, and flight tries to cover itself under the semblance of attack. A very telling illustration of this is to be seen on the battlefield. Occasionally, a soldier who is afraid and wants to run, will run, but he runs head-on against the enemy. He forsakes all normal and natural precaution for a suicidal attack which on rare occasions is successful but which normally puts an end to his fear and himself. His impulse is to deny his fear and yet to put an end to the situation which produces the fear. And so he ends it all by running away from himself but towards the enemy. This is not courage but fear. True courage holds its ground and moves forward or backward only with wisdom and precaution, but fear is always impatient and cannot wait.

The man who is not afraid is a patient man. He does not feel that life is robbing him, and that he must, with haste and impatience, get his share of its pleasures and profits while he can. The impatient man is impatient because he is afraid, because he feels that every moment that fails to bring him his hopes, that delays his expectation, constitutes a double robbery against him, a robbery of time and substance. His fear of losing out on life makes him impatient of God and man and ready to run headlong into retreat or injudicious attack. But, whether we attack or retreat, we run away from ourselves when we are impatient. Moreover, we run away also from the providence of God and attempt to institute our own special man-made providence as a safer recourse.

PATIENCE IS AN ACT OF FAITH AND A RESULT OF COURAGE. AN INDICATION OF TRUST AND FEARLESSNESS. PATIENCE DECLARES TO THE LORD. "BECAUSE THOU ART MY GOD. I WILL TRUST AND NOT BE AFRAID."

Patience is an act of faith and a result of courage, an indication of trust and fearlessness. Patience declares to the Lord, "Because thou art my God, I will trust and not be afraid." Paul declared (Rom. 5:1–5) that the believer is subjected to testing and tribulation, that it might work patience, "and patience, experience; and experience, hope: And hope maketh not ashamed; because the love of God is shed abroad in our hearts by the Holy Ghost which is given unto us." In other words, before we can have any true hope, any godly hope, God must produce patience in us, and patience comes only through testing, out of trouble and in the face of stress and strain.

It is as simple as this: to be afraid is to be impatient.

To be without fear, is to be patient. The word of the
Lord to the prophet Joel was this: "Fear not ... rejoice in
the Lord your God ... And I will restore to you the years
that the locust hath eaten" (Joel 2: 21, 23, 25).

Bradford Torrey's hymn gives us excellent guidance
here:

> Not so in haste my heart!
> Have faith in God, and wait;
> Although He linger long,
> He never comes too late.
> He never cometh late;
> He knoweth what is best;
> Vex not thyself in vain;
> Until He cometh, rest.
> Until He cometh, rest,
> Nor grudge the hours that roll;
> The feet that wait for God
> Are soonest at the goal.
> Are soonest at the goal
> That is not gained with speed;
> Then hold thee still, my heart,
> For I shall wait His lead.
> (Bradford Torrey, "Not So in Haste, My Heart," 1875.)

ARE YOU AFRAID OF GOD?

September 13, 1955

Good morning, friends. I would like to have us take a candid look at our fears and see what they tell us. Now, there is no evading the fact that we have our fears, and that while some of them are healthy, many of them definitely are not.

Scripture tells us that, "The fear of the Lord is the beginning of wisdom" (Prov. 9:10). This fear is a healthy one: it is the result of drawing near to God and thereby seeing more clearly what He is in His holiness and we, in our sin. But there is also an unhealthy fear of God which we find in people who are running away from Him. A prominent contemporary psychologist has shrewdly observed of himself and his friends that most of them do not believe in God, but that they are all afraid of Him. This is exactly right. All unbelief and atheism is a fear of God and a running away from Him; it is the terrified cry of men who insist that the thing they fear must not exist, and cannot be real, and therefore it is not. All unbelief and atheism is wishful thinking. It is an attempt on the part of man to change life because he himself refuses to be changed. Do you reveal your fear of God by denying Him?

There are other ways in which men show their fear of God. Jonah was afraid of God and so took a ship to Tarshish, vainly seeking to escape Him. The Lord had asked him to go to Ninevah and preach to that city, and Jonah refused: he had no desire to see the Assyrians saved and the Lord's blessing extended to them. Life had to be on his terms, not on God's, and so he ran away. He was afraid of what God is and does, and could not face up to it, because the plain implication was that not God but Jonah needed to give ground and be changed. If you are evading or running away from life, people, or any problem in your life, it is because you are afraid of God and what He wants you to do, and to do with you.

> THIS FEAR IS A HEALTHY ONE: IT IS THE RESULT OF DRAWING NEAR TO GOD AND THEREBY SEEING MORE CLEARLY WHAT HE IS IN HIS HOLINESS AND WE, IN OUR SIN.

But this is not all. Adam and Eve were afraid of God when they answered Him, and therefore they passed the blame, shifted the responsibility and evaded their guilt. "The woman did give me, and I did eat," said Adam. "The serpent did give me, and I did eat," said Eve (see Gen. 3:12–13). Whenever we blame someone else for our condition, our shortcomings, our failures, our sin, we are running away from God and from His truth. We are afraid of God because He exposes us and reveals that the root of the problem, the source of the evil, is not elsewhere but in ourselves.

When we fear God and run from Him, we quickly find ourselves afraid of all things. A falling leaf causes us to tremble. We distrust everything because we sense intuitively that all things testify to their Creator. We know in our hearts that there is no hiding place down here, because nowhere in all creation is there any escaping the Creator or the great and resounding witness of creation to Him. Everything in heaven and earth rejects the man who rejects his Creator. Run to the farthest corner of creation, lock yourself into the tightest closet and plug up your ears, and the mighty testimony to the Creator and His judgment will well up out of your very being. When the disciples sang their praises to Jesus Christ, God incarnate, the Pharisees demanded that they be silent, but He replied, "I tell you that, if these should hold their peace, the stones would immediately cry out" (Luke 19:40). Not only so, but when men seek to stifle their creaturehood, their flesh and their bones cry out to the Creator.

There is no running away from God. In everything, He confronts us. All men who fear God and run from Him find their flight futile. Sooner or later we must meet Him, and we meet Him either naked and afraid in our guilt and shame, or we meet Him triumphantly, clothed in the righteousness and holiness of Jesus Christ. When we meet Him in Christ, we meet Him as our Father; we meet Him in that perfect love which casteth out all fear (1 John 4:18); we meet Him, not as aliens and strangers, but as members of the commonwealth of grace, recreated in His image and made sons and heirs of His glory. Then, no longer afraid of God, our hearts cry out, Abba, Father, as we enter into the joy of the Lord.

ARE YOU AFRAID OF LIFE?

September 20, 1955

Good morning, friends. Our fears tell us something about ourselves; they indicate our strength and our weakness, our health and our sickness. Some fears are a sign of moral and spiritual health; others indicate a diseased spirit.

One particularly common and unhealthy fear is the fear of life. Ask yourself this question: "Am I afraid of life?" What does it mean to be afraid of life? For one thing, it manifests itself by a retreat from life in all its phases. The person who is afraid of life enjoys none of it. Childhood is a sorry memory, youth a painful process best buried and forgotten. Maturity means only a rash of problems, and middle age is haunted by the shadow of death, while old age brings only resentment at having been robbed of a life he or she never lived. Such is the reaction of the person who is afraid of life.

What does it mean to run away from life, to be afraid of it? It means a fear of being alone, lest life confront us with itself instead of a multitude of things. It means driving oneself to work beyond all sensible measure, because we are afraid to stop working, unwilling to face up to our responsibility to live. It means a refusal to work, because work gives meaning, purpose, and direction to life. It means an unwillingness to play, because rest and play require us to reveal a joy in life.

To be afraid of life is to be afraid also of death. The people who strive so energetically to run away from life are also most panicky in their fear of death. All their fear seems to be most vividly aroused at this particular point: life for them may be fearful, but death is even worse.

Why the strange contradiction here? Why is it that the person fearful of life does so greatly fear death instead of regarding it as a release or an escape? The reason is a clear-cut and obvious one: the person afraid of life and death is afraid because he has a sense of guilt. This sense of guilt brands him like the mark of Cain and makes him restless and homeless throughout his life. He is afraid because both life and death mean a meeting with God and the obligation of repentance and regenerated life. He knows that it is futile to face life or death without God, and because he spurns God, he can face neither.

Our generation, with its excessive lust for security, indicates thereby that it fears life and wants to find its joy and security, not in life, but in things. Our generation hopes to enjoy life after certain material things are

> OUR GENERATION, WITH ITS EXCESSIVE LUST FOR SECURITY, INDICATES THEREBY THAT IT FEARS LIFE AND WANTS TO FIND ITS JOY AND SECURITY, NOT IN LIFE, BUT IN THINGS.

achieved, and this is a tragic fallacy. Things can be
bought on the installment plan, and after so many
payments, we have full title to them. But life does not
come to us on any installment plan: we do not begin
to get life as we advance our possession of things. New
cars, houses, clothing, furniture, and silverware bring us
no closer to life but can take us away from it. We either
enjoy life, or we don't. If we enjoy life, we love it even
in its tragedies and heartbreaks, and all of it adds up
to final good for us. But if we fear life, its tragedies are
unrelieved horror, and its best moments clouded and
burdened. The sense of guilt erects a barrier of searing
fire between us and life. We are driven away from life,
even as Adam and Eve were in their sin, when the Lord
"placed at the east of the garden of Eden Cherubims,
and a flaming sword which turned every way, to keep the
way to the tree of life" (Gen. 3:24).

How can the fear of life be overcome? It cannot be
overcome by any frenzied attempt to live. We never find
life in living it, but only in God. We return to the tree of
life in Jesus Christ, by dying to ourselves, by accepting
the verdict of guilty to which our souls give witness, and
then finding forgiveness and new life in the Lord. The
answer, then, is to be reconciled to God in Christ, and to
yield Him our lives in consistent obedience. Then the joy
and abundance of life is given to us, and all of life is rich
in both promise and fulfillment. "I am come," said Jesus,
"that they might have life, and that they might have it
more abundantly ... I am the way, the truth, and the life"
(John 10:10; John 14:6). Sin and death separated man
from the tree of life; Jesus Christ restores us to it.

ARE YOU AFRAID
OF THE PAST?

September 27, 1955

ood morning, friends. *The American Mercury* this past June (1955) carried an unusual article by Peter Hewitt entitled, "Adventure in the Agony Column." Hewitt tells the story revealed in a series of advertisements in the personal column of the London *Daily Telegraph*. Every indication is that the strange items were authentic and gave compelling evidence to some grim tragedy of the last war.

It seems that three men of authority and one woman survived after fourteen weeks adrift on a float in the Indian Ocean. The horrors of those weeks left all of them scarred to the heart of their being, anxious all of them for one thing, that each one of them forget the thing completely. They made a compact to forget, to remember each other only by nicknames, never thinking of their real identity, and to make no attempt thereafter to contact each other. The woman's nickname was Sea-Wyf, the men's Bulldog, Biscuit, and Laurie.

After their rescue, nine years of silence followed. Then on March 7, 1952, one of the men, Biscuit, attempted to reestablish contact with Sea-Wyf. His second advertisement, on March 12, read, "Sea-Wyf: Have returned with fatted calf but no unsuitable memories. Please get in touch. Biscuit." As the weeks passed, the other men urged Biscuit to abide by the compact to forget, and Sea-Wyf also. He pleaded, however, for a chance to see her again, and she finally agreed only to this, to see him from a hiding place as he passed through Berwick Market. This was done, and then she ended the episode with this note in the agony column: "I came. I saw you once more which was the thing I wanted. Remember me as I was when the smoke appeared on the horizon. Goodbye, Sea-Wyf." Then came Biscuit's farewell, and final silence.

> ALL FEAR OF THE PAST IS LIVING GUILT AND ANXIETY: IT DOES NOT DECREASE AS THE PAST GROWS REMOTE: IT FEEDS LIKE A PARASITE ON ALL OUR TODAYS AND TOMORROWS.

Why have I dealt at such length about this episode? Because it tells the story of a grim and tragic past, and of only one of the participants therein being able to face that past. The obvious fact is that the woman and the three men could never forget those fourteen weeks: their dread lest one should revive any part of it testifies to the fact that they were very much alive to that past. In fact, they were afraid of that past. Biscuit had become the only member of that group on the raft who no longer feared the past and therefore did not fear the future. This fact is of central importance: if we are afraid of our past, we are afraid of our future. If there are skeletons in yesterday's closet, there will be ghosts on tomorrow's path. If we stumble over our past, we will limp into our future. The plain fact is that fear will not stay put: if it was there yesterday, it will be here today and tomorrow: it will go where we go, walk where we walk, sleep where we sleep, and dream in our dreams.

All fear of the past is living guilt and anxiety; it does not decrease as the past grows remote: it feeds like a parasite on all our todays and tomorrows.

Are you afraid of the past? Are you living under the burden of your yesterdays and in living fear of them? Then listen to the words of Warfield and Harnack, as they re-echo an ancient and fundamental Christian doctrine: "Christian happiness consists in comforted remorse." This is another way of saying that Christian happiness means the forgiveness of sins. When our sins are forgiven and blotted out by God in Jesus Christ, and only God can fully forgive our sins, then we are no longer afraid of our past, no longer haunted by guilt, no longer plagued by anxiety. Because there is now no condemnation from God, we are freed of self-condemnation and made victorious over the condemnation of men. We are no longer afraid of the future, because we have faced our past and been made victorious over it through Jesus Christ. What others fear to face, we now find our joy in: for us, the past, the present, and the future are in the hand of God, and we know Him now in His goodness. This is our victory in Christ, and this is our confidence: for if God be for us, who can be against us?

FEAR AND THE PRESENT

November 1, 1955

Good morning, friends. Some people find it
difficult to settle down and to do the business of
everyday living because they are fear-ridden and
thereby hamstrung. The simplest daily chores are an
overwhelming burden, and a tremendous effort of will
is required to settle down to the simple obligations of
life. Perhaps what is required of them is an ordinary
and routine responsibility; they know that it must be
done, and that other people do it without a moment's
hesitancy. They know that if they fail to do it, or if they
defer it, the matter will only haunt them, only add to the
burden of their already burdened lives, and yet they find
it most difficult to face up to their responsibility.

Such people are afraid of the present, of the here and
now. They postpone, defer, evade, fight shy of any and
every demand for responsibility and action on their part
because they are afraid of the present, of today, and of
this very hour. For them, the clock is always stroking out
the unhappy summons, "The time has come, the time
has come." The clock's ticking reminds them, "This is the
hour." They live constantly in the shadow of apocalyptic
doom and are too paralyzed with fear to face up to life's
common responsibilities. Their whole world is tense with

expectancy. The mailman, the newspaper, every contact is loaded with the burden of expectancy: something is on the way, perhaps escape but almost certainly the end.

PEOPLE WHO ARE AFRAID TO FACE UP TO THE PRESENT ARE PEOPLE WHO ARE AFRAID TO FACE UP TO THEIR RESPONSIBILITY.

These people can never live in the present: they insist in living in the past and in the future. Because they are guilt-bound people, they are past-bound. All their yesterdays are more real to them than their todays. Whether they interpret the past as happy or unhappy, they are past-bound and guilt-bound. They are in a fearful prison of their own making. Physical chains can easily be broken for them by others, but the chains of sin and guilt are of the spirit, and they can be broken only as man faces himself in the sight of God and finds grace and forgiveness in Jesus Christ.

Not only are such people past-bound, but they live in the future also, avoiding the present. They look to the future hopefully as a source of all good. Somehow, tomorrow must become a Garden of Eden for them to compensate for all their yesterdays and todays, and to give them what they believe they deserve.

People who are afraid to face up to the present are people who are afraid to face up to their responsibility. No man ever evades responsibility: every evasion only haunts him all his days and grows more grievous in its burden. The Lord demands an accounting, and no man renders up his tally according to his own tastes and his own dishonest numerics. The demanded accounting is not limited to Judgment Day, nor is it merely an annual audit: it is a moment-by-moment affair, and to evade our responsibility at any point means increasingly dishonest bookkeeping in our lives thereafter.

The only way any man can successfully and triumphantly live in the present is to face up to his responsibility under God. And yet no man can render a perfect accounting to God: no man can successfully discharge his God-given responsibility to the point where he puts God in obligation to himself. The only answer to this dilemma is for man to confess his sin and guilt, his failure to meet God's requirement, and to accept Jesus Christ as his God-given substitute, the atonement for his sin, who in His person discharges our responsibility and by His regenerating work in us makes us free in conscience and responsible in our living. When we face up to our responsibility, recognize that we have sinned, and seek the grace of God and become members of Jesus Christ, then the present is not something to be evaded but an area of triumphant living. Then indeed we go "from strength to strength" and appear before God as victors. "O Lord of hosts, blessed is the man that trusteth in thee" (Ps. 84:7, 12).

FEAR AND TRUTH

November 15, 1955

Good morning, friends. Fear has many faces and assumes many forms. To deal honestly with our fears is difficult, because it involves dealing honestly with ourselves.

One striking form of fear is claustrophobia, the fear of being confined, the dread of being cooped up in a little space. Some people have a great horror of being hemmed in and shut up and often find it an impossibility to endure any situation tending thereto.

There is a very real sense in which men feel a strong sense of claustrophobia when confronted by truth. To face the truth concerning themselves or to stand up for the truth in any and every circumstance is for them a fearfully confining thing. Truth gives them a sense of claustrophobia.

For the natural man, the old Adam in us, the world is always a happier and freer place if truth can be avoided. The old Adam finds it much easier to live peaceably with a lie because it is much more at home in it. We are always much more at home on familiar ground than in strange and unfamiliar surroundings, and this is true both physically and psychologically. For this reason, the old Adam loves darkness and hates the light.

For this reason, the old Adam in all men yearns for the old familiar security of a lie.

Adam in the beginning refused to acknowledge the truth of his nakedness and rebellion and chose to protect himself with a lie. In like manner, the old Adam in us cannot stand for truth without fearing judgment. All evasion of truth is an evasion of decision or judgment and a vain hope for peace in a lie.

But there is no rest, saith my God, to the wicked. For the man living in flight from truth and under the cover of a lie, there is only an avenging conscience and a nagging guilt. The straight and narrow way of truth seems thick with troubles, but it proves to be strong with a power not our own. The broad and easy way of the living lie, on the other hand, proves to be increasingly confining and tends to destruction.

> THE TRUTH SEEMS DREADFULLY CONFINING, BECAUSE IT REQUIRES THAT WE COMMIT OURSELVES, AGAINST OUR OWN PERSONAL INTERESTS, TO THE REQUIREMENTS OF GOD AND HIS WORD.

The question is thus again one of security. Can anything ever give security, short of God and our obedience to Him? Can we ever hope to find any lasting peace or security in our subterfuge and evasion, in any wishful thinking or fancied practicality? The truth seems dangerous to men because it involves a trust, not in our own devices but in the providence of God. The truth seems dreadfully confining, because it requires that we commit ourselves, against our own personal interests, to the requirements of God and His Word. In other words, the requirement of truth is that we stand when necessary against ourselves because God's commandment has priority over our needs and wishes. And this we can only do by the grace of God and through Jesus Christ, because it goes completely against the grain of the old Adam in us. If the Son shall make us free, we shall be free indeed, and part of that freedom is liberty from the bondage of a living lie, liberty from the obligation to find our sinful security in evasion and flight. We know ourselves, and we know that in us is no good thing, that our new life is in Christ and in His power. Knowing this, in God we trust, and in Him is our security.

FEAR AND THE FUTURE

November 22, 1955

Good morning, friends. When a man is ruled by fear, he is unable either to live in the present or to face the future. His days are marked by a continuing inability to face up to the reality of time and an unwillingness to enjoy life today. His life is lived, not in the real world, but in a realm of fantasy which has no relationship to causality and even less to the truth concerning himself.

Such a man is constantly dreaming about an ideal future, one in which all burdens are removed, all problems solved, and all responsibility replaced by pleasure and undeserved reward. All such people daydream glowingly about the future, but actually they are afraid of both life and the future, because they are unwilling to come to terms with themselves as creatures under God. Fantasies about the future often assume a tremendous political importance, of which Marxist Communism is an especially obvious contemporary example. The Marxist dream of a stateless, crimeless, sinless, trouble-free world is the fantasy of sick men who are afraid of the divine truth concerning themselves and are trying to create a world where cause and effect do not prevail and where God does not exist. And their fantastic creed appeals only to men who, like themselves, are trying to evade judgment by outlawing it, and trying to escape the truth concerning their wretched sinfulness by calling themselves righteous and their works the deeds of supermen. Nothing, however, can hide the fact that they are proud and angry sinners, trying to evade the wrath of the righteous God.

> IT IS BETTER TO LIVE IN TROUBLES WITH THE TRIUNE GOD THAN TO LIVE IN THE DISEASED LUXURY OF DREAMS BEGOTTEN OF ORIGINAL SIN.

Because such men cannot face the truth concerning themselves, that they are sinners before God, they cannot face anything in honesty or in truth. They cannot accept causality, for it declares that what a man sows, that shall he reap, and the wages of sin is death. They cannot face the present or the future, because both confront them with consequence, and for man the sinner all consequence is death and judgment. Thus they find refuge in fantasy, in a dream world where the sinner takes paradise and the righteous are given over to damnation.

All such dreaming is an escape from the world of time and causality, and all such evasion is a running away from ourselves. And all such attempts to escape facing up to ourselves are born of sin and involve an attempt to evade the fact of man's sin against God. The only result of this evasion is fear and more fear.

Only the man who sees himself as a sinner in the

sight of God and lives by the grace of God and in the
salvation of Jesus Christ can face himself honestly and
without flight. Only the consistent Christian can live
with himself, for in so doing, he now lives with the new
man, even Jesus Christ. Only the consistent Christian
can live readily and victoriously in the real world, in
terms of causality, in terms of time, past, present, and
future, because he alone has escaped judgment in Jesus
Christ and has victory even in death. He alone finds
the real world more wonderful than the dream world,
because he knows that God rules and prevails in the
real world, but that in the dream world it is his sin-sick
nature which is at work and in power. And it is better to
live in troubles with the triune God than to live in the
diseased luxury of dreams begotten of original sin.

The consistent Christian alone can face any and
every day, no matter what it may bring, and say, "This is
the day which the Lord hath made; we will rejoice and
be glad in it" (Ps. 118:24). This is the true faith, to live
with reality, victoriously and confidently.

FEAR AND MAN

November 29, 1955

ood morning, friends. One of the deadliest of fears is the fear of man. It paralyzes the conscience and rules the heart, mind, and being of most men. Day by day, the world capitalizes on this fear in order to bring men into submission to the law of the pack, sometimes euphemistically called the will of the majority.

Men think and live as the mob dictates. When styles are changed by the pack, the individual all too often complies. When certain opinions, faiths, and men become unpopular, the individual too often follows the mob. The crowds that on Palm Sunday hailed Jesus of Nazareth as Messiah and Son of David, their King and Redeemer, before the week's end cried out in savage blood lust, "Crucify Him! Crucify Him!"

When the mob sacrifices God the Son to its lawless whim and crucifies the Lord of glory, jeering and mocking Him in His dying agony, it cannot be expected to be merciful to mere man or to any follower of the Lord it despises. The power of the mob is real, and the power of the mob is deadly. It is devoid of any and all morality, of all faith and principle, and of all decency. The mob has usually ruled in history, and its rule has always been destructive and evil. The mob operates on one and

> **THE POWER OF THE MOB IS REAL, AND THE POWER OF THE MOB IS DEADLY. IT IS DEVOID OF ANY AND ALL MORALITY, OF ALL FAITH AND PRINCIPLE, AND OF ALL DECENCY.**

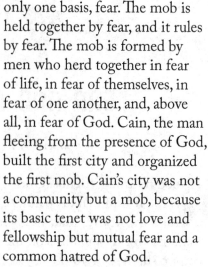

only one basis, fear. The mob is held together by fear, and it rules by fear. The mob is formed by men who herd together in fear of life, in fear of themselves, in fear of one another, and, above all, in fear of God. Cain, the man fleeing from the presence of God, built the first city and organized the first mob. Cain's city was not a community but a mob, because its basic tenet was not love and fellowship but mutual fear and a common hatred of God.

Ask yourself this question: Am I a member of the mob? Every person who is afraid of man is a member of the mob. No evasion, no contempt for his fellow men, no denial can ever change this fact: every person who is afraid of man is a member of the mob.

If you are afraid of people's opinions and criticisms and allow them to sway you, you are afraid of man, and that fear makes you a part of the mob. If you are afraid to stand for the truth because you fear that men will destroy you for it, and you keep silent, you have joined the mob. If you allow the fear of man to guide and determine your actions at any point or in any area of your life, you are a member of the mob, and may God have mercy on your soul.

Every person on the face of this earth who is ruled by the fear of man rather than the fear of God is a member of the mob. Where do you stand in all this?

The only alternative and answer to the fear of man is the fear of God. If we are afraid of transgressing the Word of God, afraid of sinning against Him, afraid of being disobedient to Him, then we will not allow the fear of man to rule us. Whom do you fear most, man or God? Are you a member of the mob or a member of Jesus Christ?

Scripture tells us that the fear of the Lord is clean, enduring forever (Ps. 19:9). It strengthens man's soul against the day of adversity and fills him with the power of God and His Spirit. It gives to man the joyful and victorious faith that sings in Psalm 118, Luther's favorite chapter:

> The LORD is on my side; I will not fear: what can man do unto me? The LORD taketh my part with them that help me: therefore shall I see my desire upon them that hate me. It is better to trust in the LORD than to put confidence in man. It is better to trust in the LORD than to put confidence in princes. This is the day which the LORD hath made; we will rejoice and be glad in it. Thou art my God, and I will praise thee: thou art my God, I will exalt thee. O give thanks unto the LORD; for he is good: for his mercy endureth for ever. (Ps. 118:6–9, 24, 28, 29)

FEAR AND EVIL

December 6, 1955

ood morning, friends. There is an undercurrent of fear in our generation which paralyzes man and increasingly clouds his days and hours. This fear has many faces, and one of its manifestations is the fear of evil.

For man today, nothing stands secure. The very ground he walks on seems unsteady to him. Andre Gide gives us what is unquestionably an extreme case and yet one most revealing of our day, when he writes in his *Journal*:

> I know a man whom a single thought sufficed to plunge into deepest melancholy, the single thought that, in the near future, he would have to buy a new pair of shoes to replace those on his feet. This man's case should not be considered one of avarice; what he felt was a sort of distress at not being able to stand on anything lasting, definitive, absolute. (C.F. Ramuz, *What Is Man*, p. 45)

This man's experience has a very real kinship to a common experience of our time. Most men feel that nothing is certain any more. They feel lost in a meaningless world, and if they believe in God, yet He remains vague and inactive as far as they can see. The one sure thing for them is evil. The evil they see and feel seeping into all of life is nothing so old-fashioned as death and taxes. It is a nameless dread and terror; it is an emptiness which seems destined to be filled only with horror; it is a waiting, a long and unrelieved waiting which evil and only evil will fulfill. For modern man, Satan is more real than God, and hell more real than heaven; after all, he already lives there and finds it therefore a simple matter to believe in it. He may hope and hunger for something better, but what he actually expects is that the bottom will drop out of everything. For him, life is like that.

> MOST MEN FEEL THAT NOTHING IS CERTAIN ANY MORE. THEY FEEL LOST IN A MEANINGLESS WORLD, AND IF THEY BELIEVE IN GOD, YET HE REMAINS VAGUE AND INACTIVE AS FAR AS THEY CAN SEE. THE ONE SURE THING FOR THEM IS EVIL.

And this gives the clue to the meaning of this fear of evil. For such people, life is like that; it is basically destined to issue in evil, because the only real power in their lives is evil. The natural man has no goodness in him. The power in his life is his bent to sin, his radical drive to sin and death. Since this is the only power he knows in his life and experience, it is the only real power he can imagine at work in the world. Men are afraid of evil when evil is the only power at work in their lives.

The only way that fear of evil can be overcome is for

man to know the power of God unto salvation. When we know the power of God to destroy sin and death in us, we know also His ability to destroy its power in the world. When we know God as our Creator and Redeemer, we know Him also as the absolute Sovereign over all things. Nothing in all creation has any meaning or existence apart from Him. We know that since every fact in creation is a created fact and therefore has meaning only in terms of the will and purpose of God, then evil has no meaning in any immediate or ultimate sense apart from the eternal counsel of God.

This fact makes the ground beneath our feet marvelously secure, because the very earth is the creation of God and can only witness to His glory and serve His purpose. Instead of insecurity, we live, move, and have our being in the security of God and His will. We can undergo all things through Christ, who strengthens us, because we know that He is the captain of the whirlwind and the storm. All our waiting is on God, and it is characterized by hope and security. In any and every circumstance, we have this assurance: our God is with us. We can say with David, "Yea, though I walk through the valley of the shadow of death, I will fear no evil: for thou art with me" (Ps. 23:4).

FEAR AND DEATH

December 13, 1955

Good morning, friends. Thus far in my ministry, one of the fears I have rarely heard confessed is the fear of death. On the contrary, I have often heard people declare, and the people who so speak are seldom Christians, that they are not in the least afraid to die. One would think, therefore, that few people are afraid of death, since so few admit to such a fear.

Actually, of course, the situation is far different. The majority of people are very definitely afraid of death. Now, in a sense this is understandable. Normally, no one enjoys dying. Scripture speaks of death as "the last enemy," one over whom we have victory now in Jesus Christ, and an enemy that shall be destroyed at the end. Sin and death alike stand in a position of enmity to man and are alike to be feared in their power, and to be fought in Christ, lest they have dominion over us.

But there is another kind of fear of death which is not honest about itself, is unrealistic, and definitely unhealthy. Many people try to act as though death were not real. Others seem to feel that it will become unreal if they never speak about it. A good many people try to run away from it with frenzied activity which only brings them that much closer to death.

> **ONE OF THE INTERESTING AND REVEALING FACTS ABOUT PEOPLE WHO ARE AFRAID OF DEATH IS THAT USUALLY THESE SAME PEOPLE ARE AFRAID OF LIFE.**

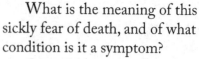

What is the meaning of this sickly fear of death, and of what condition is it a symptom?

One of the interesting and revealing facts about people who are afraid of death is that usually these same people are afraid of life. That person who evades the full meaning and purpose of life as God has destined it, and is afraid to meet the responsibilities of life, is also usually afraid to meet the responsibilities of death. To be victorious in death, we must first of all be victorious in life. As a pastor, I have been often with the dying, and the impressive thing to me is how beautiful and even joyful can be the death of those who die in the Lord. Their last days reveal a victory that leaves a blessed peace with those who stand by. And in every instance behind those hours stands a consistently victorious life.

The question, therefore, becomes the more basic one: Are you afraid of life? Are you afraid to meet its responsibilities under God? Are you afraid to be obedient, afraid to be joyful, afraid to be sorrowful, afraid to be a man or woman and confess to your fears and weaknesses that the Lord might give you strength? Are you afraid to be afraid? Until we confess to our fears, our sins, and all our shortcomings, the Lord will not remedy our ills, nor will He remove our fears. The beginning of Christian strength is humility in all things, and as

we approach the Lord in humility, confessing our sin
and our fear, He gives us righteousness and makes us
increasingly unafraid.

The Lord wants us to enjoy our lives in Him, to meet
with confident faith and humble reliance on Him all
that He sends us. Just as true marriage is for better or
for worse, "in plenty and in want, in joy and in sorrow,
in sickness and in health," so is all successful living. It
receives life in all its fullness from the hand of God,
confident that His bond of love with us in Jesus Chris
is our sure and certain ground of victory. Being unafraid
of life with Him, we become unafraid of death in Him.
With Paul, we can say, "O death, where is thy sting? O
grave, where is thy victory? … But thanks be to God,
which giveth us the victory through our Lord Jesus
Christ" (1 Cor. 15:55, 57).

FEAR AND VIOLENCE

October 17, 1955

G ood morning, friends. One of the most significant facts of our age is the constant concern with violence. When we have admitted all the defects of our times, we must still recognize that ours is a more peaceful era than most as far as the average man is concerned. The wilderness of nature has been driven back; our modern life has conveniences and well-policed security. The ravages of war are quickly eliminated by technological efficiency, and life has more security than man has usually known.

And yet men reveal both a great fear of violence and an eager interest in it. First of all, there is a tremendous interest in violence. Film, radio, TV, novels, magazines, especially murder mysteries, feed the popular appetite for violence. If there seems to be increasing violence in the world at large, remember this, that what people enjoy in their imagination, they will inevitably try to enact in their lives. If men have an appetite for violence in their reading and listening, they will create a world which centers on violence. If a person dreams continually of eating hamburgers and malted milks, you can be sure that they will consume a goodly amount of both. If a person's taste and imagination runs to violence, then they will sooner or later gratify that impulse. The interest in violence is an indication of an appetite for violence.

THE MAN WHO TRULY TRUSTS IN THE LORD IS NOT AFRAID OF VIOLENCE, NOR DOES HE REQUIRE IT IN HIS LIFE OR IMAGINATION.

And yet the fact remains that these same people are afraid of violence. Their whole world is haunted by fears of force and terror. Behind every bush and in every shadow is a nameless dread. The world is more peopled with horror than with men, and no hiding place is secure against this fear of violence. Every trip means the fear of an accident; loved ones can hardly be trusted out of sight lest the horror overtake them; the house is always likely to burn down over their heads, all of nature has a grudge against them, striving to undo them not only with earthquake, hurricane, and cyclone, but with its very sun, rain, and fog, its nights and days.

Such people fear violence, and yet they constantly open the way for it. They are most likely to leave the gas burning, the doors unlocked, the iron on, the brakes unchecked, the car mechanically unsound. They fear violence with all their being, and yet they leave the door open to violence. Why?

The first man to fear violence was Cain, who feared that every man's hand was against him, and who felt that he must be a constant fugitive and a wanderer to escape from violence. Cain feared violence because he was a guilty man before God and recognized that punishment was due him. The man who fears violence is afraid because he is guilty before God and is running away from his Almighty Judge. In his frantic flight, he finds all of God's creation to be his enemy. Heaven and earth witness against him because they witness to the Creator.

And yet, because in his heart he knows that he deserves condemnation, he constantly leaves doors unlocked to violence, hoping by his suffering to atone for his guilt. Men are constantly trying to atone for their sin and guilt by holding up their own suffering before God, refusing to realize that there is no value whatsoever in their sin-sick torment and rejecting all the while the atoning work of God in Christ. It was the suffering and death of Jesus Christ which alone brought atonement for the sin of man, and only our acceptance of that sacrifice for us can deliver us from the fear of violence and the compulsion to and necessity for violence.

The man who truly trusts in the Lord is not afraid of violence, nor does he require it in his life or imagination. Having been truly reconciled to God, he has peace with God, with his neighbor, and with himself. As David said, "In the Lord put I my trust: how say ye to my soul, Flee as a bird to your mountain?" (Ps. 11:1). The man of God can face life, because his trust is not in life, but in the Lord. He can face violence, because he knows God is on His throne. He can face himself, because he knows that God in Christ has forgiven him and given him new life in the Beloved. This is the inheritance of the faithful, and their peace stands not in men or in events, but in the faithfulness of God.

13

FEAR AND FLIGHT

October 25, 1955

Fears are a constant tattletale and a ready giveaway of many grimly held secrets in our lives. Many people keep a futile watch on their lips while their fears scream their secrets from the housetops.

Fear often disguises itself, but the disguise is never successful, and usually more revealing. One common disguise is flight. The most obvious form of flight is Cain fleeing from the face of God and man, fleeing when none pursued, because his own fear and guilt drove him into running. But flight often takes more sophisticated forms.

We are familiar with the kind of person who doesn't believe in going to doctors. Their cousin Prunella went and was six years in getting out of bed. All doctors, to hear them talk, are quacks and murderers, and a person is a fool to go near one. And, of course, they certainly would never go near a psychiatrist; such doctors are, to hear them talk, the most dangerous kind of characters. As they tell it, psychiatrists have no function but to lie in wait for innocent people, to pervert them with wild and evil theories. Or perhaps it's churches they are opposed to. According to such persons, the churches are the biggest collection of hypocrites, frauds, thieves,

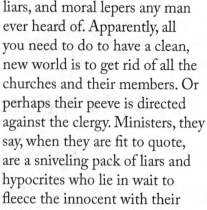

FEAR IS MAN'S CONSTANT SHADOW AS LONG AS HE LIVES APART FROM GOD.

liars, and moral lepers any man ever heard of. Apparently, all you need to do to have a clean, new world is to get rid of all the churches and their members. Or perhaps their peeve is directed against the clergy. Ministers, they say, when they are fit to quote, are a sniveling pack of liars and hypocrites who lie in wait to fleece the innocent with their gross deception. And so on.

Now, the obvious fact is that these people cannot really believe what they are saying. They know that while some doctors and psychiatrists may be incompetent, and some churches and ministers hypocritical, by and large the standard is one of integrity, usefulness, and a devotion to truth.

Then why this smokescreen of wild and thoroughly irresponsible talk? The answer is clear-cut: the whole of it is an attempt to disguise their fear and their flight. They will not admit that the truth is that they are afraid of both life and death, and thus hate any doctor who might tell them that their sickly life is ebbing away by calling attention to their ailments. They hate psychiatrists, because they are running away from God, and they resent having an institution or a person remind them of the God they try to evade.

When people start condemning these things, we can be sure that they are afraid, and that they are running away from rather than facing up to their sickness and their fear. They love their sickness, and they want neither

God nor man to challenge it.

Fear is man's constant shadow as long as he lives apart from God. He cannot escape it: it dogs him night and day and is the inevitable result of living in separation from God. No false gods that man can fashion and worship can erase that shadow: they only increase it. Let him give himself ever so zealously to his false worship, and the only result is a deepening of the shadow. There is no escaping God for all our fleeing.

There is no escaping God unless we turn and make our refuge in Him who is our Creator, unless we turn to Him on His own terms in Jesus Christ, unless we find repentance and remission of sins in the Lamb slain from the foundation of the world, even Jesus Christ our Lord. In knowing ourselves for what we are, and in finding grace and healing in God, and in knowing Him for what He is, this is our peace and our respite from fear.

"We will not fear, for God hath willed His truth to triumph through us."

(Martin Luther, "A Mighty Fortress Is Our God," ca. 1527)

14

FEAR AND MAN

November 8, 1955

Good morning, friends. In any discussion of fear, one of the most pertinent aspects of the problem is commonly omitted. People fear many things, but one of the most common sources and objects of fear is man himself. The fear of man is a common fear and a deeply rooted one.

It manifests itself in a variety of ways. Men who are not afraid to die tremble with fear and work themselves into a lather over facing other men, or standing up to them on some issue. The whole business of keeping up with the Joneses involves a deep-rooted fear of what people might say or think. I have heard people say, "I'd die if people knew this," and yet they had no hesitation in committing the acts which they feared to have exposed.

This makes clear what is involved. Such people are not particularly troubled about what God declares, or what their conscience requires, but they do fear public exposure. Thus for them the most important factor in life is not God but man, not a clear conscience but a clean social impression. What they worship, therefore, is not God but man.

A man's gods are basic to his life and existence, and what a man worships, that he fears to offend. And, above all, it is basic that a man maintain continuous communion with his god. Since his whole life depends upon his god, he cannot live except in total dependence upon him and in communion with him. Now, if our god is man, or society, then we are afraid to offend him and afraid to do anything that might break

A MAN'S GODS ARE BASIC TO HIS LIFE AND EXISTENCE, AND WHAT A MAN WORSHIPS, THAT HE FEARS TO OFFEND.

our contact with him. It then becomes more important for us to meet the requirements of human society than the standards of the Christian God. It becomes basic to our life to maintain human communication at all cost, because our communion is with man, not the Christian God. We change our standards and our tastes with the fashions of the time, because we dare not risk broken communion with our human god. Thus, if we are afraid of man, it is clearly because man has become our false god. We need to ask ourselves conscientiously: Of whom am I truly afraid, of God or of man? Whom do I fear to offend, human society or Almighty God? If it is not Almighty God whose disfavor we fear most and whose broken communion we dread, then our faith is either defective and needs to be mended, or it is false and needs to be changed.

Solomon long ago observed, "The fear of man bringeth a snare: but whoso putteth his trust in the Lord shall be safe" (Prov. 29:25). To worship the will of man is to put ourselves in a position of total insecurity, and to establish ourselves in uncertain sand. But to fear God is to ground our lives in His unchangeable and omnipotent power and to have that glorious communion which turns our weakness into strength and our sorrow into joy. As Solomon further said, "The fear of the Lord tendeth to life: and he that hath it shall abide satisfied: he shall not be visited with evil" (Prov. 19:23). The evils that beset him shall not endure, and the final outcome of his life will be victory. "The fear of the Lord is the beginning of wisdom: and the knowledge of the holy is understanding" (Prov. 9:10).

FEAR AND CHANGE

October 11, 1955

Good morning, friends. In this haunted age of ours, we find men slow in faith and ready to fear. It sometimes seems as though the very air some people breathe is tainted with fear, so that their life's blood is fed on uncertainty and the contagion of doubt.

Fear is manifested in a variety of ways. Some people are abnormally afraid of change. Most of us, of course, feel some regret as things and circumstances familiar to us and loved by us modify and change. The old order passes, and, with it, a part of our lives. But, over and above this, there is that unhealthy fear which resists any and all change because it finds its weak and sickly security in things as they are. The prophet Isaiah, before his great temple vision, found his security in the often weak, heretical, and leprous King Uzziah. Uzziah's fifty-two year reign at least gave the nation a measure of stability, however insecure that stability was. But, in the year that King Uzziah died, Isaiah, in his temple vision realized that God's purpose was the destruction of that security in order to accomplish His plan and produce true security. Too often, men cling to any and everything to fight change, because they fear change, and their fear is a witness to their lack of faith and their insecurity.

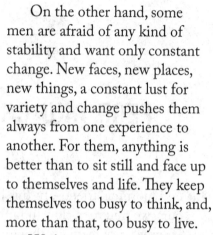

WE HAVE TWO VERY DIFFERENT KINDS OF PEOPLE, THOSE WHO HATE CHANGE AND THOSE WHO LOVE IT, AND YET BASICALLY THEY HAVE ONE THING IN COMMON, FEAR.

On the other hand, some men are afraid of any kind of stability and want only constant change. New faces, new places, new things, a constant lust for variety and change pushes them always from one experience to another. For them, anything is better than to sit still and face up to themselves and life. They keep themselves too busy to think, and, more than that, too busy to live.

We have two very different kinds of people, those who hate change and those who love it, and yet basically they have one thing in common, fear. Both are motivated by fear, both are demanding false securities of life, both have this above all in common: they are afraid to accept life as it comes to them. They are afraid to face up to life, because life changes, and also because with all its changes the basic issues of life remain the same. Samuel Moffett has pointed out that the invention of the atom bomb no more changed the nature of man and his basic problem than did the invention of the bobby pin. Man's basic problem is this, that he must recognize that he is not God but a sinner, that his only salvation is in God through Christ, and that life in all its sameness and variety comes from the hand of God. If we have an unhealthy fear of anything in life, then we are afraid of God who gives us life. If we place our hope on stability or in change, then we are trying to avoid the purpose of God behind these things. God confronts us through every event of our lives and in all its manifestations with a demand that we receive all of life from His hands. Our attachment must be, not to life's yesterdays or to life's changes, but to the God who gives us all of life's yesterdays and todays, its changes and its permanencies, and gives them for one purpose, to strengthen us in Jesus Christ and to prepare us by means of life for the fullness of life. The only preparation for life is life, and the only way to live life honestly and faithfully is to live it in Jesus Christ, who is the way, the truth, and the life.

If we love God, then we will love and enjoy life, because we know that it comes from His ever-loving hands. As John said, "There is no fear in love; but perfect love casteth out fear: because fear hath torment. He that feareth is not made perfect in love. We love him, because he first loved us" (1 John 4:18–19).

16

FEAR AND SUPERSTITION

October 4, 1955

Good morning, friends. All of us are familiar with the variety of superstitions held by many people. The rabbit's foot is considered by some to be a good luck charm, while others use medals and coins as their protective device. Spilling salt is considered bad luck, and must be nullified, it is held, by throwing a pinch of it over one's left shoulder. From the time of the Greeks and Romans, it has been believed that a sneeze is a dangerous sign to be counteracted by a quick statement, in those days of, "Jupiter preserve you," or in ours, "God bless you," or, "Gesundheit," "Good health." Breaking a mirror is supposed to be especially dangerous in its consequences, while a horseshoe can supposedly bring good luck. And so on and on, all around the world: every nation, continent, tribe, people, and tongue reveal a variety of superstitious hopes and especially superstitious fears, because the essence of superstition is fear. Even the supposedly lucky charms reveal this aspect of fear: they protect the person from surrounding dangers and threats which threaten to overwhelm him.

Superstition is fear, and this is precisely why superstition is so unreasonable. If the superstitious man loses faith in a particular charm, he replaces it with another, because the fear remains, and protection in some manner or form is an inescapable necessity for his life.

What are superstitious people afraid of? Why this overwhelming fear, and this demand for some kind of protective device? The reason is a clear and simple one: the superstitious man believes that he lives in a world or universe which is basically hostile, if not evil, and definitely out of any reasonable control. He faces a world of brute facts which menace him and concerning which he can do nothing; therefore, he needs protection, and he gets protection from the very world he fears, in the form of potent symbols of natural forces.

THE SUPERSTITIOUS MAN BELIEVES THAT HE LIVES IN A WORLD OR UNIVERSE WHICH IS BASICALLY HOSTILE, IF NOT EVIL, AND DEFINITELY OUT OF ANY REASONABLE CONTROL.

The superstitious man may say that he believes in God, but his god is a little god and a weakling. Most of the universe is out of his control, and he is unable to protect man from the consequences of this unregulated and demonic universe. If the superstitious man is right about the universe, we cannot blame him for being afraid. When modern thinkers tell him that the universe evolved itself and is its own law, then he has every reason to be afraid, because in the name of science he is given a world without mind, heart, or conscience, a world without purpose and righteous control. Modern

man therefore is very superstitious; he goes in heavily
for horoscopes, trying to find lucky loopholes in the
universe, and for liquor, trying to escape the hopelessness
of a world that makes no sense. Modern unbelieving
philosophy and scientific thought only increases the
fear of man, because they only bring man closer to the
brute forces and demonic power of a universe without
rationality or purpose.

The only answer to superstition and fear is the
sovereign God who is maker of all things visible and
invisible, by whom all things come to pass, who is the
Creator and therefore the interpreter of all things and
therefore gives meaning to all in terms of His sovereign
and omnipotent decree. There are no brute facts in
this universe, nor any blind and uncontrolled forces.
God has created all things and governs all things, and
nothing has any meaning apart from Him. We cannot
interpret a single fact in all creation apart from the
Creator, for apart from Him nothing has any existence
or meaning. Therefore, all things must be interpreted in
terms of the total providence of God. When all things
are interpreted in terms of their Almighty Creator, it
becomes apparent that when we walk as members of
the body of Christ, all things have a blessed purpose for
us: all things, whether immediately good or evil to us,
are actually mediated to us through the will of God and
thus made to work together for good (Rom. 8:28). We
can therefore say with Paul, "If God be for us, who can
be against us?" (Rom. 8:31). But if we are not living in
the fear of God, we fall into the fear of things, into the
fear of a purposeless universe and a meaningless life. The
only defense against superstitious fear, therefore, is to be

able to say in the fullest sense of the word, "I believe in God the Father Almighty, Maker of heaven and earth; and in Jesus Christ His only son our Lord" (the Apostles Creed).

17

HOW TO BE A FAILURE

PART 1 - DO AS YOU PLEASE

September 1, 1953

Good morning, friends. Let's consider briefly a matter that bothers me quite a bit. It seems to me that one of the things people work hardest at is how to be a failure. Most people spend their lives dodging work and responsibility and work harder at avoiding work than they ever do at their job.

It seems to me that this is one reason why so many people avoid Christ and His church: they seem afraid that the Lord might make a success out of the mess of their lives. After all, it's a matter of clear-cut statistical evidence that Christians on the whole have happy homes that endure, children who are loving and successful, and more satisfying and rewarding lives. Apparently most people don't want that, because they're very busy doing the things which produce failure and frustration.

If that's what you want in life, I'd like to give you a little help towards that end, so that you can be a failure more easily and quickly. There's no point in wasting time in this matter: if you want failure and frustration, you might as well get it quickly and efficiently.

The two easiest ways to failure are these: *first*, do as you please, and, *second*, be sure to blame everyone and everything except yourself for everything that goes wrong.

Let's look at the *first* easy step to failure and frustration. It's one of the easiest things in the world to say that, when you were young, your folks made you do too many things, and so now you plan to do exactly as you please. You can act very wise and self-righteous about that. After all, you're entitled to some freedom in life, you can say, and the world owes it to you. Of course, all the while you are doing as you please, be sure that you insist that your wife or husband, your children, your friends, and neighbors, do exactly what they are supposed to do, rather than what pleases them. If you persist in this course of action, you'll fail very quickly and effectively.

The *second* step to failure and frustration is to blame everyone and everything except yourself. If you blame your heredity or environment, you can do it in good style: it's all so scientific and logical. After all, sociologists have written weighty books to demonstrate how heredity, society, economics, cultural factors, education, and other factors can determine our lives.

> WHEN INSTEAD OF PLEASING OURSELVES, WE TRY TO PLEASE GOD FIRST OF ALL, THEN OTHERS IN HIM. IT'S SURPRISING HOW QUICKLY OUR SENSE OF FAILURE GIVES WAY TO PEACE AND JOY EVEN AMIDST TROUBLES.

It's really getting quite respectable to blame our failure on these factors. Or, if you don't want to make it quite so complicated, blame your boss, or your husband, or your wife. Tell yourself how wonderful you are, and how successful you would be if only your spouse were not the irritating failure he or she is: it's a wonderfully quick way to fail, and also have a good rousing fight while you're doing it.

But be sure never to blame yourself for anything. Always find someone else to blame, and let them know it. Failure and frustration will come very quickly this way.

But perhaps you're different and don't want to fail. Perhaps you don't enjoy frustration and unhappiness, as most people seem to. Then the *first* thing for you to do is to recognize that our purpose here on earth is not to please ourselves but to please God. The chief end of man, says the Westminster Shorter Catechism, is to glorify God and to enjoy Him forever. The whole purpose of our lives is to say no to ourselves and yes to the Lord. It is only as we deny ourselves and die to ourselves that we begin to receive peace and joy, and begin really to live.

The *second* step is to take full responsibility for every failure and confess it before God: to say with David, "Against thee, thee only, have I sinned, and done this evil in thy sight" (Ps. 51:4). We need to say, in the words of an ancient prayer: "Lord, I have sinned, in thought, word, and deed, through my fault, my own fault, my own most grievous fault: wherefore I pray Almighty God to have mercy upon me, to forgive me all my sins, and to make clean my heart within me."

When instead of pleasing ourselves, we try to please

God first of all, then others in Him, it's surprising
how quickly our sense of failure gives way to peace
and joy even amidst troubles. And when we accept the
responsibility for our actions and our frustrations, we
sometimes find quickly how much love and response we
gain from those whom we once blamed. But, whether we
get these practical results or not, we have this assurance:
peace with God and success in Him. God never fails,
and when His Spirit reigns in our hearts and lives, we
have a perfect guarantee against failure and frustration.
Then:

> The Lord is thy keeper: the Lord is thy shade upon
> thy right hand. The sun shall not smite thee by day,
> nor the moon by night. The Lord shall preserve thee
> from all evil: he shall preserve thy soul. The Lord
> shall preserve thy going out and thy coming in from
> this time forth, and even forevermore. (Ps. 121:5–8)

HOW TO BE A FAILURE

PART 2 - BLAME EVERYONE BUT YOURSELF

September 16, 1953

Good morning, friends. I'd like to return this morning to a matter we were discussing two weeks ago, on how to be a failure. The *first* step is this: do exactly as you please, but expect everyone connected with you to do what they are morally supposed to do; and, *second*, be sure to blame everyone and everything for all that goes wrong in your life. Always find someone else to blame, and be sure to let them know it. Failure and frustration will come very quickly this way.

Most people apparently want failure, because they do these things almost exclusively. We who want to avoid defeat and inner insecurity take a different course: *first*, we recognize that our purpose here on earth is not to please ourselves but to please God; and *second*, we take the full responsibility for all our sins and shortcomings instead of blaming others.

There is a *third* recipe for easy failure and inner defeat that I'd like to discuss this morning. We don't usually recognize independence of nature as a disease of the soul, but it is one. It's easier for us to see dependency as a sickness. The parasite whose theme song is that the world owes me a living is obviously and clearly a moral failure. But, then, so is the man who says, I owe no man anything, nor am I in the least way indebted to God. As one pathetic man expressed it some years ago,

> I am the master of my fate:
> I am the captain of my soul.

(*Invictus*, by William Ernest Henley)

Paul expressed our human situation much more honestly when he wrote, "For who maketh thee to differ from another? and what hast thou that thou didst not receive? now if thou didst receive it, why dost thou glory, as if thou didst not receive it?" (1 Cor. 4:7). In other words, everything we are, we owe to our forefathers, to our time in history, and to God. We did not choose to be born with the particular mind and body we have, or in the country and age we were born in. We had nothing to do with any of these things. We are simply a product of our inheritance and have a deep and unbreakable debt to our past, and supremely to God, who gave us life.

The independent self-made man is a person trying to live in a vacuum, in a world of his own creation. He denies his debt to both God and man. This independent spirit is no new thing. We first encounter it in the evil one, who declared of old, "I will ascend into heaven ... I will be like the most High" (Isa. 14:13–14). The demonic temptation from the beginning has been this: *to be as God*, to be independent of God and man, and a law unto oneself.

The world is full of such people. For them, there is no God and no law except their own will and their own lust. They will steal, lie, murder, covet, and commit adultery at will, if they can do so successfully. There is for

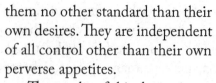

> WHEN WE TRY TO RULE ON THE THRONE OF OUR LIVES, WE FIND OURSELVES A HELPLESS VICTIM TO OUR OWN APPETITES.

them no other standard than their own desires. They are independent of all control other than their own perverse appetites.

The marks of this demonic will are frustration, inner insecurity, and a consistent sense of failure. Such men are in constant torment and for that reason have a perverse desire to pass on their torment to all around them. Mark well the man who makes a declaration of independence from Almighty God, for the end of his ways are death.

When we try to rule on the throne of our lives, we find ourselves a helpless victim to our own appetites. Pride, covetousness, uncleanness, evil-speaking, anger, lust, and hatred, and the whole train of vices take control of our lives. We try to rule independently of God and man and find ourselves controlled by our own lusts and increasingly helpless before them.

Then we resist ourselves, and cry out, "I have no king but Christ, O King of Peace, come and reign over me. O Lord, come quickly and reign on thy throne in my heart." When we make this surrender of our independence, we find release from this slavery to ourselves. We become free in Christ, and our failure turns to an unfailing and unchanging success. "If the Son therefore shall make you free, ye shall be free indeed" (John 8:36).

What is your condition today? Is it in the barren and

hopeless slavery of independence from God, or is it the freedom under God, the privilege of sonship, and the knowledge that an unfailing God lives and rules in your heart?

Remember this: if you rule over your own life, all you have at your command is your own feeble and frail power. But if Christ rules over you, then you have at your disposal all the protection, power, and unfailing success of the King of the Universe. We have this because:

> God is our refuge and strength, a very present help in trouble. Therefore will not we fear, though the earth be removed, and though the mountains be carried into the midst of the sea ... The LORD of hosts is with us; the God of Jacob is our refuge. (Ps. 46:1–2, 11)

> Be still, and know that I am God. (Ps.: 46:10)

> Ye fearful saints, fresh courage take,
> The clouds ye so much dread
> Are big with mercy, and shall break
> In blessings on your head.

> Blind unbelief is sure to err,
> And scan His work in vain:
> God is His own interpreter,
> And He will make it plain.

> ("God Moves in a Mysterious Way," William Cowper, 1773)

Remember this: if we remain in Christ, as long as God is God, we can never be forsaken.

HOW TO BE A FAILURE

PART 3 - WORRY

September 22, 1953

Good morning, friends. Last week we were discussing independence of nature as a sure and easy means to failure. The man who says I owe no man anything, nor am I in the least way indebted to God has the continual frustration of having nothing more to rely on than his own sorry self. The independent man who rules over his own life apart from God has nothing more at his command than his own feeble and frail power. But if Christ rules over us, we have at our disposal all the protection, power, and unfailing success of God Almighty.

This morning I'd like to discuss another easy step to failure and frustration. There is no easier road to trouble and defeat than *worry*. As someone has aptly stated it, "Why pray, when you can worry?" After all, prayer might solve your problems, but if you nurse your worries carefully, they're bound to increase and multiply. Go at it conscientiously and carefully and you'll be sure to lose some sleep over your troubles. Worry some more, and your digestion will be affected, and you might even develop ulcers. Keep it up, and all your friends will know that you really are worried—and they'll feel sorry for you—from a safe distance.

WORRY COMES WHEREVER THERE IS A LACK OF TRUST IN GOD. AND IT MEANS FRUSTRATION AND INNER FAILURE.

The man who worries is bound to fail sooner or later because he has a bigger problem locked up in his head than anything life can bring him. Some years ago, a man living on the edge of town felt very miserable about the neighbor's rooster, which had a habit of crowing towards sun-up every morning. He had a beautiful home, an excellent income, a young and beautiful wife, a circle of famous friends, in fact, everything to live for, but he worried himself sick over that crowing rooster, until he became a burden to his friends, a pain to his wife, and, above all, a torture to himself. When he protested bitterly to his poor neighbor about the rooster, the man answered that, after all, it couldn't be too bad, because the cock only crowed three times, and then towards morning and close to the man's rising time anyway. But the rich man protested bitterly that although the crowing wasn't too bad, the waiting was what ruined him. "If you only knew," he declared, "what I suffer waiting for that cock to crow!"

That's what worrying is like. It involves a bigger problem in itself than anything life is likely to bring you. It wasn't the crowing cock that caused the trouble: it was the sick mind of the rich man who heard it.

Worry comes wherever there is a lack of trust in
God, and it means frustration and inner failure. Go
ahead and worry, if you want to fail, but remember this:
the real problem in your life is not those things which
have happened to you or might happen to you but your
own doubting heart. The biggest enemy of the man who
worries is himself. No enemy can rob him of more sleep,
poison more of his food, spoil more of his days, and
cheat him of more happiness and success than worry—
and it comes from his own mind. If you've been busy
manufacturing your own poison, it's high time you took
stock of your own life.

If there is a God, it doesn't make sense to worry, does
it? If God is God, then He is capable of assuming your
burdens, is He not? And if God indeed revealed Himself
in Jesus Christ, then we have a God who welcomes and
takes our burdens, makes all things, including evil, work
together for good for us, and in everything supplies our
needs. Is there any sense in worrying when you have a
God like Jesus Christ?

Go ahead and worry if you want frustration and
failure, but if you want the blessed peace and assurance
of God, stop trusting in your own little self and trust
in God instead. Any man who trusts in himself has
grounds for worrying, but the man who trusts in the
Lord has grounds for serene confidence. Our God is
able, and with Him nothing is impossible. When we
by faith become members of Jesus Christ, then we are
made partakers of God's unshakeable success. We know
that He will lead us safely through the deep waters of
trouble and affliction into the safety of His arms. In this
confidence we invite you to a life free from worry, to a

life in Christ, "Casting all your care upon him; for he careth for you" (1 Peter 5:7).

"The eternal God is our refuge, and underneath are the everlasting arms" (Deut. 33:27).

HOW TO BE A FAILURE

PART 4 - INDULGE IN CRITICISM

September 29, 1953

Good morning, friends. We've been spending some time this past month in discussing the ways and means of being a failure. Last week, we saw that one of the easiest roads to failure and frustration is *worry*. The man, or woman, who worries is his own worst problem. If you are a worrying person, the real problem in your life is not those things which have happened to you or *might* happen to you, but your own doubting heart. The trouble with the person who worries is this: they depend only on themselves, and any man who trusts in himself has ground for worrying, but the man who trusts in the Lord has grounds for serene confidence. His troubles are being handled to his ultimate good by a loving God.

This morning I'd like to suggest another easy road to failure and criticism. If you want to fail in a hurry, indulge in *criticism*. Criticize everything and everyone—except yourself, of course. The beautiful part of it is that once you start criticizing, there's no shortage of things to criticize. This person's nose is too long, and hers is too short. That man needs a haircut, and this woman talks too much. One person is too homely for words, and another is really stuck on his or her good looks.

One thing about being critical: nobody may love you for it, but you're bound to have an audience most of the time!

What *does* it mean to be critical? We have to go back to Adam and Eve to answer that. *They* gave into the satanic temptation, "Ye shall be as gods, knowing [i.e., determining] good and evil" (Gen. 3:5). In other words, Adam decided there was no need of bowing down to a God in heaven when every man could be his own god and decide for himself what would be right or wrong. Instead of God being the only true judge, Adam decided that he himself was the only real judge, and so he immediately began criticizing, as a false judge will do. He began by criticizing Eve as no-account, and then he criticized God for giving him such a woman.

The critical man is like that. He criticizes both God and man, because, in his own heart, he has made himself god over all. And, since he is god in his own eyes, he sets a standard for everyone to meet and spends his time judging and criticizing them because they obviously *don't* meet his standard. As a result, such a person is intolerable to live with. Absolutely nothing can ever be right unless it is done exactly as he wishes it done. He cannot tolerate the freedom and independence of anyone connected to him because he believes that he, as god in his own eyes, must be all in all to everyone else.

The critical person trusts no one except himself, because, according to his warped and demonic logic, no one else is a god except himself.

This is the meaning of the critical spirit. It is a

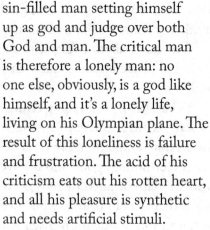

IF YOU WANT TO FAIL IN A HURRY, INDULGE IN CRITICISM. CRITICIZE EVERYTHING AND EVERYONE —EXCEPT YOURSELF, OF COURSE

sin-filled man setting himself up as god and judge over both God and man. The critical man is therefore a lonely man: no one else, obviously, is a god like himself, and it's a lonely life, living on his Olympian plane. The result of this loneliness is failure and frustration. The acid of his criticism eats out his rotten heart, and all his pleasure is synthetic and needs artificial stimuli.

The true Christian, however, avoids this failure. When Christ comes into his heart, he surrenders all claim to being judge and lord, and makes Christ his God and Savior. Instead of judging people, he now loves them. Instead of criticizing others, he forgives, knowing that Christ has generously forgiven him. The true Christian is more troubled about his own faults than the faults of is neighbor. Instead of being impatient with people, he is now patient, because he knows God has been patient with him. He sees himself, not as a little god, but as a sinner saved by grace and rejoices in the goodness of God through Christ.

He can say with Paul, "When I am weak, then am I strong" (2 Cor. 12:10). That is, when I see my littleness, then I trust not myself but the Lord. The Lord uses the humble and the weak of this world to confound the proud and the mighty. Thus the way to end failure is to humble yourself under the mighty hand of God, and

He will exalt you in due season. Then you can say with David,

> I trusted in thee, O Lord: I said thou art my God.

> My times are in thy hand …

> Oh how great is thy goodness, which thou hast laid up for them that fear thee; which thou hast laid up for them that trust in thee before the sons of men!

> O love the LORD, all ye his servants…

> Be of good courage, and he shall strengthen your heart, all ye that hope in the Lord. (Portions of Ps. 31)

HOW TO BE A FAILURE

PART 5 - BE IN LOVE WITH YOURSELF

October 6, 1953

Good morning, friends. Since so many people seem to be thoroughly bent on being a failure, we're going to spend a little more time on the ways and means of getting the *worst* out of life. Last week we saw that an easy road to failure and frustration is *criticism*. The critical person sets himself up as judge in the place of God and criticizes everyone in terms of himself. He trusts no one except himself and believes no one else is capable of doing anything exactly right. On the other hand, the true Christian loves instead of criticizing, is patient instead of impatient, and knows that the only true judge is God and not himself. Living thus in the Holy Spirit, he avoids failure and has a victorious and peace-filled life.

This morning we are going to consider a very popular way to failure and frustration, and a very commonly used one: *be in love with yourself*. A great many people need no urging whatsoever in that regard. The big love affair of their lives is exactly that: their love of themselves. It's a romance that doesn't fade away with the years but only grows more passionate and intense.

We see such people all around us—and very often in our mirror, don't we?

The person who is deeply in love with himself expects the whole world to share his passion. Everyone has to feel as deeply in love with him as he is himself. It makes no difference how he treats them: he can be nasty, suspicious, angry, thoughtless, cruel, faithless, and unloving, but if you dare doubt his love, or express any disapproval of his character, you are then a traitorous and disloyal person. We all know people like this. They are not interested in anything but their own lives, love nothing but themselves, trust no one but themselves, and yet are always afraid that everyone near them is disloyal and worthless. They are ready to lie about the most trivial matters rather than admit that their grand passion is a wayward one and that they can be wrong.

THE CENTRAL LOVE AND DEVOTION OF OUR LIVES CAN ONLY BE DESERVEDLY GIVEN TO GOD HIMSELF, AND TO HIS SON, JESUS CHRIST. EVERY OTHER LOVE WILL FAIL YOU.

What makes them so? How can people be so blind as to fall in love with themselves? The answer is again the same. At the root and basis of every failure is the old satanic temptation to be as God. Man deifies himself and his wishes and sets himself up as the center of the universe. Everything in his world has to revolve around him, since he is the heart and center of all. If he has a family and employees whom he can control, he leads them a dog's life if they fail to bow down and worship his god, himself.

The man who is in love with himself believes that he is the most important thing in the world, or else should be. He devotes his life to the only thing that matters in his world, his own welfare. He is concerned with the fundamentals of life, and he believes them to be his interests and desires.

We can agree with these great lovers on one point only: a man should love the most important thing first and foremost, but we cannot agree that the most important thing in the world is your life and mine. When you come right down to it, we really don't matter very much, except to a few, and we can be easily forgotten. There is nothing that really matters above all else in this world, nor can we even rate the world itself that high.

The central love and devotion of our lives can only be deservedly given to God Himself, and to His Son, Jesus Christ. Every other love will fail you. Your loved ones fail you, or do not understand, or they die and leave you alone. And if it is yourself whom you love, you really have no security and nothing but continued turmoil and frustration. You have peace with neither God nor your neighbor, nor yourself. But when you love God, who alone deserves your life's central devotion, then you can love others in Him. Jesus said, "Thou shalt love the Lord thy God with all thy heart, and with all thy soul, and with all thy strength, and with all thy mind; and thy neighbour as thyself" (Luke 10:27). Deep down in their hearts, people love only themselves, and others only if they please them, until the Lord changes their lives and gives them a new life, now centered, not on the self, but on the Lord. Then, because we are no longer self-centered and self-loving, we can love our neighbor. As John stated it, "We love, because he first loved us" (1 John 4:19, ASV). In other words, God shows us how to love. We don't deserve His love, being selfish and wrapped up in ourselves, but He loves us all the same. His love not only surrounds us but works through us to affect our world.

Paul said, long ago, "Set your affection on things above, not on things on the earth" (Col. 3:2). Give your love to Him who will never fail you, and you will then have peace and victorious living. Any love short of that leads to frustration, and any love apart from or outside of Him fades away. As the old hymn so beautifully states it:

O love that wilt not let me go,
I rest my weary soul in Thee;
I give Thee back the life I owe,
That in Thine ocean depths its flow
May richer, fuller be.

(George Matheson and Albert L. Peace, "O Love that Wilt Not Let Me Go.")

May "the Lord direct your hearts into the love of God, and into the patience of Christ" (2 Thess. 3:5, ASV).

HOW TO BE A FAILURE

PART 6 - DEMAND FOR PERFECTION

October 13, 1953

Good morning, friends. Last week, we were dealing with the most popular love affair of our time, man's love of himself, and we saw that one of the quickest ways to failure and frustration is to be in love with yourself. The man who is in love with himself believes that he is the most important thing in the world, or else should be. He expects the whole universe to revolve around himself and is perpetually frustrated because the world goes its own way without paying any attention to him. The Christian, on the other hand, realizes that far from being the center of the universe, he is a sinner, and a very small potato, and cannot be the center of even his own limited activity. His love must be given to God instead, and, loving the Lord with all his heart, soul, strength, and mind, and his neighbor as himself, he finds joy and peace in service to the true center of all things, God Himself.

This morning, let's look at another easy way to failure and frustration, the demand for perfection. We've all seen people who demand an impossible standard of perfection from everyone connected with them. Their children must be exactly so, and the poor youngsters are pulled this way and that and molded into a conformity with some wild standard their parents have. They have no life of their own: the only thing that matters is that they be exactly what their parents wish them to be.

Or perhaps it is a wife who expects perfection of her husband. She is constantly ashamed of him and bitter because he is everything but perfect, and is really nothing more than another man, with nothing more than the usual failings and defects of men. As far as she is concerned, he has to be the perfect husband, the ideal lover, the constantly attentive and devoted man, or her attitude is, "Heaven help you, you poor worm, if you fail to be perfect!"

Sometimes it's the husband who makes such demands. His wife has to be beautifully groomed at all times, even when she is doing the wash or scrubbing the woodwork. The children must always be neat and respectful, the house spotless, everything running by the clock, while he sits back and enjoys it all.

There's one thing we can say about these persons who demand perfection: they are about as far from perfection themselves as a person can be. Such people are always complaining that their loved ones have let them down, without ever realizing that they themselves are responsible for their plight. Few people are more difficult to live with than they, and they fail to see their sickness.

What disease of the soul is it that leads to this intolerant demand for perfection? It is the ancient hunger in the human heart for paradise, for the Garden

> THERE'S ONE THING WE CAN SAY ABOUT THESE PERSONS WHO DEMAND PERFECTION: THEY ARE ABOUT AS FAR FROM PERFECTION THEMSELVES AS A PERSON CAN BE.

of Eden, for a world of perfect circumstances and people. Adam and Eve could not return to that perfect world because their own sin barred them from it. The perfection of paradise stemmed from a total obedience to God, but the perfection which sin-filled man hungers for is a perfection in obedience to himself and in satisfaction of his own wishes. Let all the world be good, he reasons, and all my problems will be over. The person who demands perfection is constantly unhappy and yet always hoping that tomorrow the children, the employer, her husband or his wife, will suddenly become perfect and everything will be wonderful as a result. They pin their hopes of happiness on others and fail to see that they themselves are the only ones who can give themselves happiness. The true source of happiness is a peaceful and contented heart, and the surest way to quick frustration is to look for perfection in those around us.

The Christian's happiness does not depend on a perfect world or a perfect family but on a perfect God. We have this confidence, that although we may be surrounded by overwhelming problems, unloving and ungrateful people, and undergoing very real trials, we still are in the hands of an almighty and a loving God, and He doeth all things well. In Him there is no shadow of turning, and His perfection is more clear than the light of a million suns. We have this confidence, that when we become His people in Christ, He loves us and surrounds us with His providential care. Then we can say with Paul, "If God be for us, who can be against us? He that spared not his own Son, but delivered him up for us all, how shall he not with him also freely give us all things?" (Rom. 8:31–32). And God says unto us, "I am the Lord thy God ... open thy mouth wide, and I will fill it" (Ps. 81:10). "If ye abide in me," says Jesus Christ, "and my words abide in you, ye shall ask what ye will, and it shall be done unto you" (John 15:7). This is the victory which overcometh the world, even our faith, for our God is able, and we shall not want.

HOW TO BE A FAILURE

PART 7 - BE UNGRATEFUL

October 20, 1953

Good morning, friends. For the past few weeks, we've been discussing how to be a failure. Last week we saw that an easy way to failure and frustration is the demand for perfection. These people who expect everything to be perfect are about as far from perfection themselves as a person can be. They hunger for a perfect world, but forget that the perfection of paradise stemmed from a total obedience to God. The perfection they demand is one of obedience to themselves and a satisfaction of their own wishes and dreams. They pin their hopes of happiness on others and fail to see that they themselves are the only ones who can make their own happiness. The Christian avoids this failure. His happiness does not depend on a perfect world, or a perfect family, or a perfect husband or wife, but on a perfect God who never fails.

This morning, let's look at another popular way of being a successful stinker and a failure: be ungrateful. Why bother to thank anyone for anything? After all, they ought to be glad to do things for you, since you are somebody special. Of course, people should thank you when you do something for them, because you don't owe anybody anything, and what you do for anyone is a big favor: they ought to be grateful. But us: well, people ought to be glad to do things for us.

Husbands have a habit of thinking like that at times. Why bother being grateful to the wife for anything? After all, she ought to be thankful every day that she landed somebody like him. No other woman can make that statement! Let her cook, make beds, clean house, wipe little noses, shop, mend and sew, wash dishes, and anything else she has to do. She has no kick coming. Let her pat herself on the back because she's got as good a man as God ever made, a fairly good roof over her head, loads of dresses and half-worn shoes in the closet, and about everything a woman has a right to ask for. So thinks the husband.

The wife? Is she grateful to her husband for working hard all day to support her and the family? Oh no! Why be grateful to a big lug who spends all day smiling at customers and comes home and just sits and grunts when you ask him a question or two, or three. He says, with a silly smile, "Can I help you, please?" to the women in the store, but catch him saying that to his wife!

Or children: It's always, "Ma, I want this, or, gee, why can't I go—all the kids are going," or, "I'll just die if I can't have a new dress for school." Never any gratitude, except on Mother's Day, or on a few special occasions.

They remember too late, when the parent are gone. That happens so many times. And wives—well, they don't stop to think ahead to the ten or so years that the average wife outlasts her husband—long and lonely years

> **THE TRUE CHRISTIAN IS ALWAYS GRATEFUL TO THE LORD. AND AS A RESULT. HE MEETS ALL MEN IN THAT SAME SPIRIT.**

for a widow who has nothing but her whining and nagging to remember. Ungrateful years give only sour and hapless memories. The husband was never right when he was alive, and now it's too late. He always embarrassed her then—but if she could only have a little of that humanness now. The husband, well, the richness of the years is gone, and he never saw the wealth he had at home and in his family—until too late.

We are ungrateful people, are we not? And our worst ingratitude is to God. He made us, gave us His creation to live in, forgives us our sins in Jesus Christ, and we live day after day as though He didn't exist. We act as though we didn't owe Him a thing, and yet we owe Him all of our life and all our substance. Is it any wonder we're ungrateful to each other? We neglect our biggest debt of gratitude, our gratitude to Almighty God, and to His Son Jesus Christ our Savior, and as a result are too blind to see our lesser obligations.

The true Christian is always grateful to the Lord, and as a result, he meets all men in that same spirit.

Exactly what is the Christian grateful for? Two things. *First*, he is grateful to the Lord for his creation, and, *second*, for his salvation. God gives us life, our physical life, and then eternal life for the taking in Jesus Christ His Son. We show our gratitude by giving Him the same kind of gift: the only proper response to the gift of life is the gift of our own lives to Him. Instead of failure and frustration, this act of gratitude on our part leads to peace and joy. Be anxious about nothing, said Paul, but instead, being established in the knowledge of Christ, be thankful for everything, and then "the peace of God, which passeth all understanding, shall keep your hearts and minds through Christ Jesus" (Phil 4:7).

But I will sing of thy power; yea, I will sing aloud of thy mercy in the morning: for thou hast been my defense and refuge in the day of my trouble. Unto thee, O my strength, will I sing: for God is my defense, and the God of my mercy. (Ps. 59:16–17)

The Lord is my strength and my shield; my heart trusteth in him, and I am helped: therefore my heart greatly rejoiceth; and with my song will I praise him. (Ps. 28:7)

HOW TO BE A FAILURE

PART 8 - STAND ON YOUR RIGHTS

Oct. 27, 1953

Good morning, friends. We've spent almost two months now dealing with how to be a failure, and we've seen some of the traits that lead to frustration and trouble: do as you please, blame others for everything, be independent of everyone, worry, criticize, be in love with yourself, demand perfection of everyone, and be ungrateful, and you're bound to fail.

This morning I'd like to deal with a more subtle and dangerous way to failure: stand on your rights. This seems like a perfectly harmless thing to do. In fact, to most people, it looks like the healthy and moral thing to do. After all, if you're in the right, stand on your rights, and don't budge an inch. Make the other fellow, who is obviously in the wrong, give in every time. Stand on your rights, and fight for them. To most people, there's something wrong with the man who won't fight for his rights.

Maybe so, but if Scripture means what it says, standing on your rights is a deceptive business. It gives you a wonderful glow of moral fervor and a feeling of righteousness when you are actually on the road to frustration and doom.

What do you get out of standing on your rights? Supposing your husband is dead wrong; supposing everything you're thinking about him is absolutely right. You're going to make the big lug crawl down and admit his wrong and really make up for things this time. Let's say he does do it, hating every minute of it, just because he wants peace in the family. Well, you've got your rights; but the results are a little sour all the way around, and there's less room for love.

> THE MAN WHO STANDS ON HIS RIGHTS WILL GET THEM: BUT WITH HIS RIGHTS COME FAILURE AND FRUSTRATION. HATRED AND A LOVELESS LIFE.

The man who stands on his rights will get them; but with his rights come failure and frustration, hatred and a loveless life.

Jesus never asked us to stand on our rights: He asked us to surrender them! He said, "Whosoever shall compel thee to go a mile, go with him twain" (Matt 5:41). A great many people have been puzzled and bothered by that statement, but only because its obvious meaning is so hard to take. If a man violates our rights, we, instead of saying, I won't go your way, say instead, I'll give up my rights and go the second mile with you. Most of us are unwilling to go the second mile with those we love, and here Jesus is actually insisting that we do it with those who abuse and even hate us. He does not suggest this

as a technique to win friends and influence people. His
one purpose in suggesting this course is that we might
be true and faithful children of our Father which is in
heaven.

You see, God went the second mile with us. If God
were to stand on His rights, our case would be hopeless
with Him. We've broken His commandments, have
been poor stewards of our lives, tend to love ourselves
more than we love Him. As the psalmist observed, "If
thou, Lord, shouldest mark iniquities, O Lord, who shall
stand?" (Ps. 130:3). Lord, if you should start demanding
your rights and chalking up our offenses what chance
would we have?

But God does not stand on His rights with us.
Instead, He goes the second mile, and much, much
further. It was a very long second mile from His right to
condemn us to His mercy through Jesus Christ, who is
God's second mile with us. Today, God is not standing
on His rights with us: He's walking that second mile.
How can we dare, then, to stand on our rights with
anyone? How can we claim God's mercy when we are
merciless towards each other? The second mile of Jesus
Christ for us led Him to a convict's death on the cross
on that lonely hill called Golgotha. If we have walked
there with Him, we left our rights there at the cross. We
died to our rights, and now we stand on the new ground
of grace. We know our case is hopeless on any other
ground, and we have joy in the presence that walks with
us and gives us new life.

The Lord walks the second mile with me today.
Hour after hour, He overlooks His rights when He deals
with me. I can make no claim to any righteousness of

my own: I only walk with Him, and share in His.

Who walks with you today? You and your rights in lonely frustration? Or does He walk beside you, going the second mile with you, as you do the same for others?

It's a long road ahead, and it leads to home only if the Guide be with you. He says, I will go with you. I will never leave thee, nor forsake thee (Heb.13:5). I left my rights at the cross. Deny thyself, deny your rights, take up your cross and follow me.

Why walk alone?

THE POOR IN SPIRIT

February 16, 1954

Good morning, friends. I'd like to begin a series of discussions on the Beatitudes this morning. People talk a great deal about believing in the Sermon on the Mount when they actually believe in nothing at all. The so-called simple moral faith of this great document goes very much against the kind of belief the average man has. The next time someone tells you that all they believe in is the Sermon on the Mount, ask them if they know what it means, and what it says.

What it teaches is not the moralism commonly assumed. The Beatitudes begin with the simple statement: "Blessed are the poor in spirit: for theirs is the kingdom of heaven" (Matt. 5:3). Goodspeed's paraphrase brings out an aspect of the meaning when he renders it thus: "Blessed are those who feel their spiritual need, for the Kingdom of Heaven belongs to them."

In other words, our Lord began by declaring that there is no hope for the self-sufficient. People who are satisfied with themselves, satisfied with their homemade religion, confident that this world will give them everything they want, for these people there is no hope. In fact, the very thing which the self-sufficient man despises is made the starting point of true life. Most people have no desire to confess themselves poor in spirit or to declare that they feel an aching spiritual need.

But for such people there is neither blessing nor hope. Their lack of need and their restless self-sufficiency is their doom. We are not blessed, i.e., happy, until we feel our spiritual need. Greek philosophy used to say, "Know thyself," and affirmed that man was the true measure of all things. It was believed that the more we knew and understood ourselves, the more power, wisdom, and peace we would possess. Self-knowledge led, it was believed, to self-sufficiency and strength.

> **THE BLESSED OR HAPPY ONES ARE THOSE WHO ARE DISCONTENT WITH THEMSELVES AND WHO FEEL THEIR SPIRITUAL POVERTY.**

Against all such faith our Lord issued an ultimatum: the blessed or happy ones are those who are discontent with themselves and who feel their spiritual poverty. He doesn't claim an easier life for them: He simply asserts that discontent with ourselves, with all the troubles it may bring, means also a true happiness.

We can never be content with God until we are discontented with ourselves. The Lord will never be sufficient for us, until we are no longer sufficient unto ourselves. Thus true happiness, true blessedness, means recognizing that we ourselves are the ground and source of all our misery and that there is no escaping misery and frustration until we escape from ourselves. If our lives are wrapped up in ourselves, we are trapped and caged in a very narrow room, but if we turn from our spiritual poverty to His limitless wealth, we have the liberty of God's sons and heirs.

Notice that the beatitude does not say that the poor in spirit are blessed because the Kingdom of heaven shall be theirs. It declares they are blessed because the Kingdom is theirs. The moment that we see our spiritual poverty and turn to the Lord is the same moment that makes us heirs of the Kingdom.

All self-esteem and self-complacency is banned and condemned by our Lord and is due for judgment. Scripture asserts that "the day of the Lord shall be upon all high things … and the loftiness of men shall be brought low" (see Isa. 2:12, 17). The only true starting point of religion must be that of the Beatitudes, poverty of spirit, which closes the door on self and opens the door to the Lord.

Blessedness is not something outside of us, something to be bought or borrowed. It is in us, if it is anywhere.

To recognize that we are poor is spirit is to long for the Spirit of God in our lives, and that longing is immediately answered by His presence, and the gift of the Kingdom, together with all its blessedness.

Thus, by being poor, we are made rich. By humbling ourselves, we are exalted. By dethroning ourselves, we are enthroned in Him.

We need, therefore, to humble ourselves and see our poverty of spirit and our spiritual need. In the words of an ancient divine, "Wherefore, good people, let us beware of such hypocrisy, vainglory, and justifying of ourselves. Let us look upon our feet; and then down peacock's feathers, down proud heart, down vile clay, frail and brittle vessels." As the verse puts it:

Wouldst thou be chief? Then lowly serve.

Wouldst thou go up? Go down;

But go as low as e'er you will,

The Highest has been lower still.

The humbling poverty of spirit He asks of us our Lord Himself demonstrated to all of us. That same humility becomes us all. Moreover, it is the starting point of blessedness and the key to the Kingdom. God keeps His promises, and we can rely on His work when He declares:

Blessed are the poor in spirit: for theirs is the kingdom of heaven. (Matt. 5:3)

THEY THAT MOURN

February 23, 1954

Good morning, friends. Last week we began a study of the Beatitudes and saw that the meaning of the poor in spirit is this: they are the people who feel their spiritual need, who are not self-sufficient but hunger for God. This poverty of spirit is blessed, because it is the key to the Kingdom. We can never be content with God until we are discontented with ourselves. The Lord will never be sufficient for us, until we are no longer sufficient to ourselves. Thus, by being poor in spirit, we are made rich in grace. By humbling ourselves, we are exalted. By dethroning ourselves, we are enthroned in Him.

This morning, let's look at the second beatitude: "Blessed are they that mourn: for they shall be comforted" (Matt. 5:4). Sometimes, I wish that some Christians were a little less sanctimonious, and more thoughtful: it would then produce a sounder piety. The logical thing to ask, when you hear this beatitude, and too few ask it, is this: mourn for what?

The answer becomes obvious, when we look at the Beatitudes as a whole. Blessed mourning is mourning for our poverty of spirit, for our spiritual rebelliousness and shortcomings.

After all, we do have something to be sad about when we take a good long look at ourselves. Man is sick in mind, body, and soul. He is infected with a restlessness in all things: he no sooner has a good thing than he grows weary of it. He finds it easy to hate, and hard to stay long in love with anything. We live in a world where it takes hard work to make flowers and vegetables grow, and countless millions of hours and dollars are spent each year trying to coax these plants out of the ground and into their proper maturity—but it takes no work to grow a weed. Weeds are much more at home in this world. A long time ago, a slave, who was a philosopher, Aesop by name, whose fables I read with pleasure in my school days, spent many hot and hard days in his master's vegetable patch. He found, like some of the rest of us, that with all his hard and backbreaking work, he had a better weed patch than a garden. Aesop concluded that this state of affairs was typical of life as a whole. The world wants Barabbas free, and Christ crucified: it prefers the weed, because its nature is similar to that of a weed.

You and I know that this is true of ourselves also. Our lives are good weed patches. We come by dirt naturally, but it goes against the grain to obey the Lord. We can pick a thing to pieces with pleasure, but to do good, we cannot, not without self-conscious and

> THIS, THEN, IS BLESSED MOURNING, TO SEE OURSELVES AS GOD SEES US, AND TO BE FILLED WITH GRIEF OVER THAT FACT.

laborious effort. We are always more tired on Sunday morning than on any other day of the week. It is easier for us to see a man's faults than his virtues, and more congenial to criticize than to praise—unless we're salesman. We are by nature weed patches, and any good thing planted in us has a struggle to grow and needs care, cultivation, and protection.

This is what it means to realize that we are poor in spirit, that our lives are a garden for weeds and a desert to God. This is what we are asked to mourn about.

A long time ago a statesman in the Southern Kingdom, in the court of King Uzziah, saw suddenly his poverty of spirit and was filled with mourning, declaring, "I am a man of unclean lips" (Isa. 6:5). All his brilliance, his statesmanship, his prominence had its origin in a heart and life which was unclean. Isaiah saw himself as a weed patch and was shaken to the core of his being by that fact. Isaiah saw himself, however, only when he had seen the great vision of the Lord exalted in His Temple. When we see God, then we can truly see ourselves. Self-knowledge begins with the knowledge of God. Because He created us, our lives have meaning only in terms of Him and are not understandable until we know Him.

This, then, is blessed mourning, to see ourselves as God sees us, and to be filled with grief over that fact. For such mourning, there is sure and certain comfort: we shall be comforted. He who gives us this insight into ourselves gives us with it this comfort: that He is able to produce something useful and even glorious unto Himself out of our lives. He is able to change us, to root out the weeds increasingly, and to produce a good harvest from the seed He sows.

Thus this blessed mourning is the beginning of the harvest. It is a sign that the process of weeding has begun, and that the ground is being broken and ploughed for a true sowing.

The Beatitudes describe, step by step, the growth of Christian faith and life, the birth and growth of new life. In that process, even that which hurts is blessed. As our Lord declared:

> Blessed are the poor in spirit: for theirs is the kingdom of heaven. Blessed are they that mourn: for they shall be comforted. (Matt. 5:3–4)

THE BLESSED MEEK

March 2, 1954

Good morning, friends. In going through the Beatitudes we have seen, these past two weeks, that they who are poor in spirit, i.e., who feel their spiritual need, have the promise of the Kingdom of Heaven. Blessed mourning is to see ourselves as God sees us, as sinners, as self-willed, self-centered people, and, grieving over that fact, to have the assurance of His grace and comfort.

The third beatitude is our concern this morning: "Blessed are the meek: for they shall inherit the earth" (Matt. 5:5). This is probably the best known and the most unpopular of the Beatitudes. To most people, there is something repulsive and cowardly about meekness. It suggests the crawling, cringing slyness of a Uriah Heep. Men like Nietzsche have despised Christianity for daring to exalt such a trait as meekness into a virtue. Such men, however, have only revealed their own nature in their condemnation. They have not silenced the ringing promise of those words: "Blessed are the meek: for they shall inherit the earth."

Well, then, who are the meek? Who *are* these people who shall inherit the earth in part in this life and in its fullness in the new creation?

Let's get their meaning firmly fixed in our minds: the meek are the tamed. That, literally, is the meaning of meek. Meekness does not mean a lack of spirit, but rather a wild nature that has been disciplined and tamed.

The blessed meek are those whose nature is by the inheritance in Adam wild and rebellious. Seeing their poverty of spirit, and mourning over their waywardness, they submit to the discipline of the Lord and are tamed by Him.

We can understand something of the meaning of meekness by looking at wild horses. The northern Nevada-southern Idaho country from which I moved to Santa Cruz last year is wild-horse country. My brother-in-law, a sheep man in Colorado, lives in wild-horse territory, also. Over his fireplace, he has a magnificent photograph of a trapped wild stallion, fierce, unruly, and hopelessly wild, and therefore useless. Few people realize that the average wild horse is a stunted animal. It's part of the penalty of his wildness. The average tame horse can far outperform the wild horse and is therefore useful. But the wild horse is hunted for chicken feed, or for canning for overseas consumption.

In the same way, you and I are useless to the Lord as long as we are by nature wild and untamed. The more we persist in our wildness, the more stunted we become, and the more useless. The only way we can become useful is to be broken to harness or to saddle. The breaking process is a hard and painful one. The price of meekness is a life of being broken from our ways to fit the ways of the Lord. The more we resist the breaking process, the harder we are ridden, until we accept the superior direction and respond to the reins. Meekness is thus

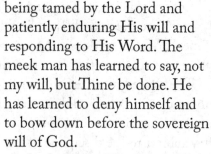

MEEKNESS DOES NOT MEAN A LACK OF SPIRIT, BUT RATHER A WILD NATURE THAT HAS BEEN DISCIPLINED AND TAMED.

being tamed by the Lord and patiently enduring His will and responding to His Word. The meek man has learned to say, not my will, but Thine be done. He has learned to deny himself and to bow down before the sovereign will of God.

In dealing with other men, the tamed man again reveals his meekness. Instead of responding to evil with evil, he obeys the apostolic commandment: "Be not overcome of evil, but overcome evil with good" (Rom. 12:21). He is patient, merciful, and forgiving in his dealings with all men. He controls his tongue, an important sign of meekness because one of the hardest things to tame is our speech. The meek life is a harnessed life, and the harnessed life is the life of power.

Thus it is that men whose lives are tamed and harnessed do flourish and prosper. To a very great extent, they do inherit the Kingdom here and now. But the fullness of their inheritance awaits them in the new creation at His coming again. Meekness has its inheritance, and it is of the Lord.

All of us need more meekness in our lives. We resist the breaking process and prefer our wildness, but in our hearts we know that our only peace is in submission to His will. If we are tamed by Him, we are heirs in Him. This is His sure and certain promise to us, for He said:

Blessed are the poor in spirit: for theirs is the

kingdom of heaven. Blessed are they that mourn: for they shall be comforted. Blessed are the meek: for they shall inherit the earth. (Matt. 5:3–5)

28

BLESSED ARE THEY THAT HUNGER AND THIRST

March 9, 1954

ood morning, friends. The Beatitudes, in giving us the conditions of blessedness, tell us *first* of all that we must be poor in spirit, i.e., we must fill our spiritual need and poverty. *Second*, we must see ourselves as God sees us as sinners, self-willed, self-centered people, and grieving or mourning over that fact, we have the assurance of His grace and comfort. *Third*, we are blessed if we are meek, and the meek are the tamed. Meekness is to be tamed by the Lord and patiently to endure His will and respond to His Word. The meek life is a harnessed life, and the harnessed life is the life of power.

This morning the fourth beatitude is our concern: "Blessed are they which do hunger and thirst after righteousness: for they shall be filled" (Matt. 5:6). The Bible urges us to be content with our place and station in life and to avoid the restlessness and fever of those who always yearn for something else. But at one point the Lord places His stamp of approval on discontent. The first four beatitudes tell us emphatically that we can never be content with God until we are discontented with ourselves.

And the fourth beatitude tells us that if we long, more than anything else, to be good in the sight of God and in His service, we shall be blessed, we shall be filled with righteousness.

The question we need to ask ourselves is this: do we really hunger and thirst after righteousness? There is a cheap answer to this question which many people give, and it's no good. They declare that they do indeed hunger and thirst for a righteous world, and we can take them at their word, but that isn't the concern of our Lord in this beatitude. I don't have to be any kind of a man at all to want a good and sound government in Washington, a righteous world, and honest neighbors. It would make my life vastly easier if this community or this world were a righteous one. A man who was, among other things, both a bootlegger and an extortioner, once complained to me about the crookedness of the people he did business with. I had no idea, he told me, how much dishonesty and double-dealing there was in the world. Now, this man was honestly concerned about the sinfulness of man. As far as he was concerned, he would have enjoyed seeing me prosper in my ministry, because he wanted to see other people turn honest. But

> IF WE LONG, MORE THAN ANYTHING ELSE, TO BE GOOD IN THE SIGHT OF GOD AND IN HIS SERVICE, WE SHALL BE BLESSED, WE SHALL BE FILLED WITH RIGHTEOUSNESS.

the hunger and thirst for righteousness which he felt was never for himself. And there is no blessedness to such a discontent.

Remember how pleased Herod was with John the Baptist's preaching. John declared that public officials should be honest, soldiers should be content with their pay, citizens obedient rather than rebellious, and the religious leaders of the day more concerned about their own waywardness than that of the government. King Herod loved these sermons of John: as far as he was concerned, they were what the country needed. But when John demanded that Herod show righteousness in his own life, especially in his marriage, then it was a different matter, and Herod lost his interest in religion and in righteousness. Too many people today, like Herod, are all for reforming the world, but will not clean up their own lives. Much preaching is of this nature also. This is not the hunger and thirst for righteousness of which our Lord speaks, and any who feel that because they are anxious to see a neighbor or friend clean up his life, or the nation become godly, that they thereby please God and meet the terms of this beatitude, are fooling themselves and are guilty of phariseeism as well.

To hunger and thirst after righteousness is to realize that we, in our own hearts, are anything but good. It means that we recognize ourselves to be rebels and sinners before God. It means that we recognize our readiness to sin, and our laziness, our only occasional desire to be better than we are. It means we understand that in our selfishness we are ready to long for riches, for domestic happiness, for promotion, for success, for everything under the sun except what we most need—

the righteousness of God in our lives. And seeing this in ourselves, we feel that hunger and thirst, and ask God to give us both that hunger and thirst and its fulfillment.

The outcome is this: we shall be filled, says our Lord, not by our righteousness, which is a lie and hypocrisy, but by the righteousness of God. He says to us, "Ho, every one that thirsteth, come ye to the waters … come to me, and drink. Him that cometh to me, I will in no wise cast out." We shall be filled: this is the promise. For:

Blessed are the poor in spirit: for theirs is the kingdom of heaven. Blessed are they that mourn: for they shall be comforted. Blessed are the meek: for they shall inherit the earth. Blessed are they which do hunger and thirst after righteousness: for they shall be filled. (Matt. 5:3–6)

29

BLESSED ARE THE MERCIFUL

March 16, 1954

Good morning, friends. We've been spending some time, these past few weeks, on the Beatitudes, and we have seen that they tell us what it is that leads us to God and gives us His blessedness. *First* of all, we must feel our spiritual need, our poverty of spirit. *Second*, seeing ourselves as God sees us, we mourn over our sins and shortcomings and deliver ourselves, by His grace, into His hands. *Third*, we become the blessed meek, i.e., the tamed or disciplined of God. And *fourth*, we hunger and thirst after righteousness, i.e., we realize that in our own hearts we are anything but good, and we need the righteousness of God. The promise is that for these things, the Kingdom of Heaven is ours.

This morning, we shall examine the fifth beatitude: "Blessed are the merciful: for they shall obtain mercy." This is probably as popular as any of the Beatitudes, and is a frequently quoted verse. One reason for its popularity is the failure of most people in understanding what is meant in Scripture by mercy.

All right, then, what is true mercy? Well, *first* of all, mercy is certainly not forgiving what is done to others. It's easy to be merciful, if you can call it that, in such cases.

A friend who visited me a few days ago got married at the end of the 1920s, a very poor young man who had only an old Model T Ford and $25 to his name. His brother, who is now a college professor, acted as best man and handled his little bankroll for him and very grandly gave most of it to the preacher. As soon as they got outside, the poor bridegroom, faced with a honeymoon on $5.00 in a Model T Ford, blew

> TRUE MERCY COMES INTO BEING ONLY WHERE WE FORGIVE WHAT IS DONE TO US... IT RETURNS GOOD FOR EVIL.

his top about the $20 fee to the preacher, but his brother protested immediately, "Well, I didn't want him to think we were cheapskates." It's easy, you see, to be generous with other people's money. Sacramento and Washington are good proof of that. In the same way, it's easy to be merciful when, not I, but somebody else is hurt. True mercy comes into being only where we forgive what is done to us. It is born out of the anguish of our own hurt and pain and extends kindness and love to those who hurt us. It returns good for evil.

Second, true mercy is not a condoning of evil. A great many people today feel very virtuously that they are displaying mercy when they are only showing spite and evil. Some people, for example, are very ready to show mercy towards a drunken murderer, and our juries seem to be full of such persons, who can be only malicious towards a good man or woman. I remember sitting in on a discussion a fine prison chaplain had with some women who were convinced that all convicts were wronged people who really had hearts of gold, and that guards and policemen were wicked and sadistic people who lived only to abuse these nice people. So many novels, short stories, and movies tend to foster the same kind of perverted mercy. And it is a perverted mercy, because what it really involves is a secret or unconscious kinship with evil and a hatred of good. This is not mercy but viciousness disguising itself as mercy. True mercy does not blur the distinction between good and evil.

Third, true mercy does not overrule justice nor is it separable from justice. A sensible parent does not say that because he or she is merciful, there must therefore be no discipline and no justice in the family. The two are inseparable. God is a God of justice and of mercy. His justice is as inflexible as His love is great. Of the two men who went into the Temple to pray, it was the publican, who was aware of the high requirements of God's justice, who was also aware of His mercy, and cried out, "God be merciful unto me a sinner" (Luke 18:13). Thus, true mercy is closely allied to justice. It means realizing our impossibility of qualifying for God's fellowship on the basis of justice, for we are sinners by nature, and relying instead on His mercy. Knowing His mercy, we live in Him and try to establish His justice in our lives and in this world. But, as we see the failure of others, we show the forgiveness we ourselves have received. We forgive as we have been forgiven. We are merciful, because He is merciful to us. Mercy is based, not on our whims and feelings, but on His Word and purpose. We are asked to show forth God's mercy and not ours, which is a warped and misguided thing. And the Lord's mercy is a blessed thing, both to him who gives it and to him who receives it. The promise to us is this: that we shall obtain mercy as we have given it. So speak the Beatitudes, declaring:

> Blessed are the poor in spirit: for theirs is the kingdom of heaven. Blessed are they that mourn: for they shall be comforted. Blessed are the meek: for they shall inherit the earth. Blessed are they which do hunger and thirst after righteousness: for they shall be filled. Blessed are the merciful: for they shall obtain mercy. (Matt. 5:3–7)

30

THE PURE IN HEART

March 23, 1954

Good morning, friends. We have been studying the Beatitudes these past few weeks and have seen something of their declaration concerning the way to God. This morning the sixth beatitude is our concern: "Blessed are the pure in heart: for they shall see God."

This is a definitely unpopular beatitude because, at first glance, it excludes us. "The pure in heart"— who might that be? Certainly none of us. Here in one sentence we are offered what we need, i.e., to see God, and with the same offer excluded by the requirement of purity.

Some moralists and philosophers, as Alexander MacLaren has pointed out, tease and mock men by offering hopes that can never be realized. They are as cruel in so doing as a man who tells a wounded soldier on a battlefield, both of whose legs are shot off, "Get up and run, and you will avoid capture, and the doctors can save your life." A great many cults and sects are safe in promising the impossible, as they constantly do, because they ask the impossible as the way to their particular dream world.

Now one thing we can be sure of: Jesus Christ was not mocking us when He promised that the pure in heart shall see God. As always, He offered only that which He was ready to give.

Let's see, then, how the heart can be made pure. *First* of all, we recognize that Scripture is right in describing the heart as desperately wicked and deceitful above all things (see Jer. 17:9). We are naturally self-centered; we worship our own desires and appetites, and we are more interested in ourselves than we are in God, the world, and all other men. Scripture, facing this tainted nature of man, asks the blunt question, "Can the Ethiopian change his skin, or the leopard his spots?" (Jer. 13:23). The answer is an obvious no. I cannot change the color of my skin or my eyes or chose to be born at some future date. I remain the same man. The only one who can change me is God Himself. He changes me by taking over my life and making it His. When I recognize and confess that I am definitely not pure in heart and can never hope to see God, Jesus Christ, having made me a member of His body, gives me His purity and His vision. I am now pure in heart, not in my self but in Christ. I can now see God, not by myself, but in and through Jesus Christ. The pure in heart, therefore, is Jesus Christ, and all who are members of Him share in His purity and its privilege before God. Every man, we are told, who has the gift of Jesus Christ, purifies himself even as He is

> **THE PURE IN HEART, THEREFORE, IS JESUS CHRIST, AND ALL WHO ARE MEMBERS OF HIM SHARE IN HIS PURITY AND ITS PRIVILEGE BEFORE GOD.**

pure. "Having therefore these promises, dearly beloved, let us cleanse ourselves from all filthiness of flesh and spirit, perfecting holiness in the fear of God" (2 Cor. 7:1).

Having therefore this purity of heart, the indwelling presence of Jesus Christ, we then see God. But what does this mean, to see God? How can a man see God, who is Spirit, whom no man hath seen at any time, nor can see? To see God seems to be a contradiction in terminology, at first glance.

But our Lord Jesus Christ Himself declared, "He that hath seen me hath seen the Father" (John 14:9). In Him, God was manifest in the flesh; in Him, the fullness of the Godhead dwelt bodily. "The Word was made flesh, and dwelt among us, (and we beheld his glory, the glory as of the only begotten of the Father,) full of grace and truth" (John 1:14). To be pure in heart, we must have Christ in us, and to see God, we must see this selfsame Christ in His glory. As MacLaren has summarized it, "We see God when we have God. When we have God we have enough."

Thus the way to receive the promise of this beatitude is threefold. *First*, we cry out as we see our impurity, "Create in me a clean heart, O God!" (Ps. 51:10). He answers, "I will give you a new heart, and take away the stony heart out of your flesh, and I will give you a heart of flesh, and I will pour clean water upon you, and ye shall be clean" (see Ezek. 36:26). *Second*, He becomes the heart of our lives and our purity, and Christ is thus our purity of heart. *Third*, having Christ, we have Him indwelling within us and opening our vision progressively to His fullness.

Thus this beatitude offers us no empty hope but rather a way of escape from our impurity and corruption to the purity, holiness, and eternal life of God Himself. By seeing our poverty of spirit and our impurity, and mourning over that fact, we are made meek, i.e., tamed of God. Filled with a hunger and thirst after His righteousness because we know the fallacy of ours, we see ourselves as God sees us, and are filled with His Spirit. We show that we have received His mercy by revealing the same mercy one to another. We can see and do these things only as Christ dwells in us, and His presence purifies and sanctifies us, and our vision of God becomes clearer.

The Beatitudes are thus vividly true in their promises when they declare:

> Blessed are the poor in spirit: for theirs is the kingdom of heaven. Blessed are they that mourn: for they shall be comforted. Blessed are the meek: for they shall inherit the earth.

> Blessed are they which do hunger and thirst after righteousness: for they shall be filled.

> Blessed are the merciful: for they shall obtain mercy. Blessed are the pure in heart: for they shall see God. (Matt. 5:3–9)

31

GOD'S PEACEMAKERS

March 30, 1954

ood morning, friends. The seventh beatitude
declares with great simplicity: "Blessed are the
peacemakers: for they shall be called the children
of God." Our concern, this morning, is to understand
the meaning of this promise.

First of all, this beatitude presupposes some kind of
activity on our part. It is not enough for us to be poor
in spirit, meek or tamed, hungering and thirsting after
righteousness, merciful, and pure in heart. Something
more is required of us, something which relates us
definitely to men and the world in our Christian faith.
We are asked to be peacemakers.

What does it mean to be called God's peacemaker?
First of all, a peacemaker is not a man who believes
in peace at any price. Such men have no real motive
in their peacemaking except this: they hate trouble
and want to avoid it, and so they adopt a philosophy
of letting sleeping dogs lie, of avoiding every possible
conflict, and of dodging every fight. There are a great
many Christians, and a great many ministers as well,
who think they are peacemakers when the truth is that
they are really afraid to fight and are merely dodging
the issues. Such men are not peacemakers but rather

troublemakers and war makers. Instead of settling anything, they allow it to build up into more and greater trouble. The peace such people seek is a weak, insecure, and beggarly thing. The true peacemaker does not dodge the issues. He faces the fact of conflict and knows that no pious folding of hands or closing of eyes will make it go away.

Second, the peacemaker brings something to the conflict. Alexander MacLaren has said, "No man can bring to others that which he does not possess," and Thomas a Kempis long ago urged us, saying, "Set thyself first in peace, and then thou shalt be able to give peace to others." If our lives are full of hatred, frustration, resentment, animosities, and pride, we can only give these things to others, never peace. And that's the trouble with much of our peacemaking: we have nothing to bring to it except ourselves. All too often, a reconciliation scene between two people, or between husband and wife, only starts a new fight because neither has anything but resentment to bring to the reunion. God's peacemakers know these things. They have seen their failure and mourned their poverty of spirit. Seeing their own failure, they have learned to be merciful towards others. Distrusting their own hearts, they have laid hold of the purity of God's Son and made it theirs. They therefore bring peace to the conflict.

The *third* question that faces us now is this: what is the peace that they bring? Scripture tells us that Christ is also called "Peace Bringer" and "Prince of Peace" because His work was that of reconciliation between God and man. "God was in Christ, reconciling the world unto himself" (2 Cor. 5:19). If all we have to bring to

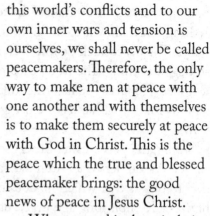

IF OUR LIVES ARE FULL OF HATRED, FRUSTRATION, RESENTMENT, ANIMOSITIES, AND PRIDE, WE CAN ONLY GIVE THESE THINGS TO OTHERS, NEVER PEACE.

this world's conflicts and to our own inner wars and tension is ourselves, we shall never be called peacemakers. Therefore, the only way to make men at peace with one another and with themselves is to make them securely at peace with God in Christ. This is the peace which the true and blessed peacemaker brings: the good news of peace in Jesus Christ.

What reward is there in being such a peacemaker? We can be sure of this, that we shall find our very effort to bring peace made a source of trouble by some. We can expect to be treated as troublemakers, rather than peacemakers, by those whose conscience accuses them and who try to cover their own inner condemnation by condemning others. The reward which men will give us for our peacemaking will be very slight, if any, but this is not the important point by any means. The beatitude promises peacemakers this: "they shall be called the children of God." This is the important point, not what man calls us but what God calls us, and when He calls us His children, we can be sure that we have a position which shall endure. We shall realize more fully, with the years and with death, the meaning of the name He gives us. We are made heirs, joint heirs with Christ, of all eternity.

This is what it means to be a peacemaker, and to receive the reward of our service. It is a disciplined life in

Christ, and a tamed and changed life. Any fool can start a fight. Any idiot can burn down a house. But not every man can reconcile fighters, nor every man build a house. To be a peacemaker requires patience in Christ, and a readiness to serve and leave the results in the Lord's hands, which is where they are anyway. The Beatitudes thus summon us to see ourselves as we are, and then give the reins of our lives and our activity to the Lord. As the popular expression has it, "Let go, and let God." It is His Son who summons us to this new life, saying:

> Blessed are the poor in spirit: for theirs is the kingdom of heaven. Blessed are they that mourn: for they shall be comforted. Blessed are the meek: for they shall inherit the earth.

> Blessed are they which do hunger and thirst after righteousness: for they shall be filled.

> Blessed are the merciful: for they shall obtain mercy. Blessed are the pure in heart: for they shall see God. Blessed are the peacemakers: for they shall be called the children of God. (Matt. 5:3–9)

"FOR THY SAKE"

April 6, 1954

Good morning, friends. We have been studying the Beatitudes these past two months and have seen that in substance they tell us this, that the keys to the Kingdom are to be had when we deny ourselves and believe in the Lord, when we say no to ourselves and yes to the Lord. We must see our own spiritual and moral poverty and mourn over it. We must become the meek or tamed men of God, who hunger and thirst for the righteousness of God, knowing that we do not have it of ourselves. We are required to be as merciful and forgiving towards each other as God is to us. To be pure in heart, Christ has to become the heart of our lives, and become our peace in order that we might give peace to others.

The last three verses of the Beatitudes deal with one final promise, the promise of trouble. This is what Jesus said:

> Blessed are they which are persecuted for righteousness' sake: for theirs is the kingdom of heaven. Blessed are ye, when men shall revile you, and persecute you, and shall say all manner of evil against you falsely, for my sake.

Rejoice, and be exceeding glad: for great is your reward in heaven: for so persecuted they the prophets which were before you. (Matt. 5:10–12)

In these words, we see the rigorous honesty of our Lord. There was no false pretense about what He offered, it was the Kingdom of Heaven, yes, but it was first of all trouble and antagonism. A good many people believe that a religion is no good unless it promises to get rid of all your problems and eliminate all troubles. And there are cults which do these things. If something bothers you, well, it just isn't there, so that cures you of any trouble. Such religion only leaves you with more trouble. It's like the poor husband who complained of a headache, and his sour wife remarked, "Listen to the man brag. You have no head." Well, I'd say the man had only a bigger headache as a result of this. You can't get rid of trouble by pretending it isn't there. Job tells us that man is born into trouble as the sparks fly upward, that is, as surely as smoke and sparks rise up out of a fire, just as certainly troubles are part of the life of men.

This is an unpleasant fact for us to face. We like to dream of a time and place when all our troubles are over and we relax and enjoy life according to our plans. But each year brings its problems and troubles, and we can no more escape trouble than we can escape from ourselves. And that, in fact, is the answer: we escape from trouble as we escape from ourselves, as we live, less unto ourselves and more unto the Lord. But the minute we escape from the old frustrations and problems of the self, we are confronted with a new kind of trouble. We face an inevitable antagonism from the world. We represent now an alien standard. We cannot accept as a true standard for ourselves or for life that whatever ministers to human needs is right, because we now declare that the only true standard is God and His Word.

Thus, what we have done is to swap one kind of trouble for another. But there's more to it than that. Man's lot is indeed trouble, but the only blessed trouble is that which is "for righteousness' sake." The grief we bring on ourselves outside of Christ is a curse, rather than a blessing, and it leaves only a lingering taste of bitterness and shame. And our Lord declares that everything we endure for His sake is blessed. Instead of being a source of grief, we can rejoice and be exceeding glad because of it, because such trouble and antagonism indicates that we successfully set forth the life and standard of the Lord. More than that, it means that we have a reward for our faith and witness which far transcends any difficulties we may encounter. We can't avoid trouble in this world, and we might as well face up to this fact. If we're going to have trouble, let's make it count and let's stand for something in the process. We will not be persecuted for righteousness' sake, unless we make a stand for it. There is a healthy peace that comes from the knowledge that when the times have come, we have stood up and been counted, that we were ready in trying circumstances to be merciful, to be peacemakers, to be men and women who could stand and defend God's truth unafraid, and,

> WE ESCAPE FROM TROUBLE AS WE ESCAPE FROM OURSELVES. AS WE LIVE, LESS UNTO OURSELVES AND MORE UNTO THE LORD.

in all things, to stand for righteousness' sake. This is the end result of our walk in God: we begin by seeing our poverty of spirit, our spiritual and moral need, and we end by standing not in our power, but in the power of God and His Christ. For this reason, we can rejoice and be exceeding glad, for the life we now live is not our life, but the life of Christ in us. And for this reason, the Kingdom of heaven is ours.

All the promises of the Beatitudes are in the future except the first and the last. Those who see their poverty of spirit and stand for righteousness have, here and now, the Kingdom of Heaven. They have in their lives the peace and power of God, because their lives now turn, not on themselves, but on the Lord Himself.

Both for what it gives us now, and promises us in the world to come, the Beatitudes are the Magna Carta of Christian liberty.

This is the promise:

Blessed are the poor in spirit: for theirs is the kingdom of heaven. Blessed are they that mourn: for they shall be comforted. Blessed are the meek: for they shall inherit the earth. Blessed are they which do hunger and thirst after righteousness: for they shall be filled. Blessed are the merciful: for they shall obtain mercy. Blessed are the pure in heart: for they shall see God. Blessed are the peacemakers: for they shall be called the children of God. Blessed are they which are persecuted for righteousness' sake: for theirs is the kingdom of heaven. Blessed are ye, when men shall revile you, and persecute you, and shall say all manner of evil against you falsely, for my sake. (Matt. 5:3–11)

33

HE THAT OVERCOMETH

May 18, 1954

Good morning, friends. There are times when many of us wish we could play God for a little while and make a few changes in the nature of things around us. We would certainly eliminate some of those very trying problems which dog our steps, and we would reach out a helping hand to friends whose grief or need leaves us distressed and normally helpless. We'd make quite a few changes towards making our lives richer and happier, and this world a safer and healthier place to live in. Our way of making these improvements would be to eliminate problems.

That, inevitably, is the solution we gravitate to and think of constantly. As far as we're concerned, life's freedom, meaning, and richness would begin as soon as those problems could be eliminated.

An obvious question then raises itself. If life can be so greatly improved by the elimination of these problems, they why doesn't God eliminate them? After all, He does have the capacity and power to do so. By His sovereign will and word, God can do anything. Then why does He permit us, year after year, to flounder about in the sickening and searing jungle of human life today?

Why doesn't He eliminate these problems and conditions to begin with?

NOT BY ELIMINATING PROBLEMS BUT BY OVERCOMING THEM DO WE GAIN PEACE AND VICTORY.

We like to dream of such a solution, and we show our weakness in this. We fail to recognize or admit that the problems we want to avoid are often more necessary to us than the peace we crave. We refuse to recognize that problems and troubles are as much God's instruments as anything else. Just as a child would like to receive all his nourishment in the form of candy, cake, and ice cream, so we want God to give us all the blessings of life without any of its problems. An intelligent parent makes certain that his child gets a healthy diet, and the God of love makes sure that we get a healthy diet of problems to develop on.

It is a great and foolish mistake for us to demand peace and victory before the battle is begun. We cannot avoid the battle without at the same time avoiding the peace and victory that follows it. Problems and troubles are a hard necessity without which life would become impossible, peace unattainable, and man without character. Our Lord promised us peace and victory, but, first of all, He declared that His work would be a divisive one. It would result in painful division, trouble between members of a family and between friends, and would separate men. "I am come," Jesus said, "not to bring peace on the earth, but the sword" (see Matt. 10:34). In short, He asserted that the way to peace and victory lay through trouble and defeat. He warned all His disciples against a peace too hastily claimed. He promised them only an inner peace, not a trouble-free or peaceable location in life. And this inner peace, He declared, would sustain them in all things. Not by eliminating problems but by overcoming them do we gain peace and victory. Therefore, God does not eliminate all our problems but very often adds to them in order that He might truly bless us.

Jesus declared (John 12:24) that a grain of wheat must fall into the ground and die in order to bring forth fruit. In the same way, you and I have to die to ourselves in order to live in Him. All the problems of life are an assault on our ego, on the old Adam in us, trying steadily to drive us out of ourselves, our constant source of trouble, into the hand of God, our only source of peace and strength.

Jesus said, "To him that overcometh will I grant to sit with me in my throne, even as I also overcame, and am set down with my Father in his throne" (Rev. 3:21). Our Lord gained His peace and victory by overcoming, and we ourselves need to realize that peace is the portion only of those who overcome in Christ. We are told that "he that overcometh shall inherit all things" (Rev. 21:7). This is a call to struggle, with the assurance of His power in the battle and His peace at the end.

More than that, this declaration contains an important promise concerning our inheritance. The Swiss poet C. F. Ramuz has declared, "Man never has what he wants, because what he wants is everything. It was/is only in God that he could/can have *everything.*" The promise definitely carries the clear-cut statement that everything is due to the man who overcomes in the Lord. The time shall come, in eternity, when the redeemed man shall inherit all things. Meanwhile, we walk in this confidence, that our problems are God-given and will be used to our ultimate peace. As Cowper's hymn declares:

> Ye fearful saints, fresh courage take;
> The clouds ye so much dread
> Are big with mercy, and shall break
> In blessings on your head.

(William Cowper, "God Moves in a Mysterious Way," 1773)

THE ROAD TO PEACE

February 9, 1954

Good morning, friends. One of the subjects of major interest to people in our time is peace, both political and military peace, and peace within. In fact, the very word "peace" seems to be an important factor in selling books. If the word appears in the title, such as *Peace of Mind*, and *Peace of Soul*, it adds to the market value of the book, because millions of people are restless and at sea. One thing they definitely do lack is peace. They may have a good home, a fairly good bank account, and many of the securities you and I may long for, but they definitely do not have peace.

Well, these millions of people have a very sensible desire for peace. Their restlessness of mind and disquiet of soul is a constant drain on them, and it leaves them always frustrated. So they buy the books, read them, get a temporary glow out of them, and then tuck them on a shelf. And the old frustration returns, as soon as the book is out of sight.

You can't blame them, therefore, if they feel irritable when someone starts preaching peace of soul to them again. The whole business sounds like so much ministerial quack medicine talk. I think there's some truth to that suspicion in some cases. I myself am inclined to be suspicious with no disrespect to the books of that title, if someone starts preaching this peace of mind and peace of soul business to me.

After all, how much sense would it make if someone started telling me that there was nothing for me to do to get $100 every Friday or Saturday night, except to say I'd sign on the dotted line and affirm my conviction in the value of $100? I'd say there was a catch someplace between Monday and Saturday, a catch involving forty to forty-eight hours of hard work before that money was mine. And unless the world has changed a lot overnight, I think I'd be right. The only way I've ever gotten money is by hard work. I'd like an easier way, but I haven't got one.

> WE DON'T GET PEACE OF MIND OR SOUL SIMPLY BECAUSE WE WANT IT. WE GET IT AS THE RESULT OF HARD AND SACRIFICIAL WORK. WE GET PEACE AS A PAYCHECK WE'VE HAD TO EARN.

The same is true of peace. We don't get peace of mind or soul simply because we want it. We get it as the result of hard and sacrificial work. We get peace as a paycheck we've had to earn.

Our Lord, speaking of peace and like blessings, said, "He that overcometh shall inherit all things" (Rev. 21:7). In other words, before we get peace, we do some overcoming, some fighting. When we make the mistake of choosing peace instead of facing the struggle, we fail to win peace, and we inherit only tension and frustration.

As old Abraham Kuyper observed, "Woe to the man who reaches after peace, before the battle shall have been fought."

And so this paradox is true: peace comes only with struggling and overcoming. It involves especially a struggle with ourselves. We desire peace in order to save and protect ourselves. But our Lord said, "The corn of wheat which falls into the ground and dies, brings forth fruit" (see John 12:24). In other words, we have to die to ourselves to have peace. Well, that sounds like a bitter dose at first. A graveyard is indeed a peaceful place, but not exactly the kind of peace we have in mind. But what our Lord offers is not a graveyard peace, but the peace of joy and faithfulness in Him, bringing forth fruit to Him, that is, love, joy, peace, longsuffering, gentleness, goodness, faith, meekness, and self-control (Gal. 5:22–23). This involves saying no to ourselves daily, and saying yes to the Lord. It involves loving our neighbor and our enemy. It means forgetting ourselves in service to God and to others. Peace is a paycheck we earn in payment for a struggle with ourselves. It is our dividend for turning over the title deed of our lives to Jesus Christ. To make our peace with God, Jesus Christ had to lay down His life for us, and He exacts in return the payment of our lives to Him in return for this gift.

Christ is our peace (Eph. 2:14), and to the extent to which we allow Him to prevail in our lives, to that extent we have peace. A man's heart is surrounded by nettles, fencing it off from any touch or trampling, but only as they are ripped out and overcome by God's grace can he have that peace which passeth all understanding (Phil. 4:7).

And let the peace of Christ rule in your hearts, to which indeed you were called in the one body. And be ye thankful. (Col. 3:15, RSV)

Now the Lord of peace himself give you peace always by all means. (2 Thess. 3:16)

HOW TO LIVE WITH YOURSELF

PART 1 - SELF-CONDEMNATION

November 10, 1953

Good morning, friends. A very real problem for too many of us is this: how to live with ourselves.

Most people seem to find it difficult to live with themselves. They find it very hard to be alone or to have nothing to do. But most of all, they find it difficult to keep from judging themselves.

One man, for example, makes a boner in the course of his work, or fails in a pinch when everyone expected him to succeed. He goes home grousing about it, broods all evening, tosses and turns half the night, and faces the next day only half awake and hating himself for being a failure.

Or perhaps it's a woman who says something out of turn and goes home burning with embarrassment. She moans and groans, "If only I'd had the sense to keep my mouth shut." And all night long she relives the situation, thinks of all the really brilliant answers she could have made and never thought of until much later. "All I ever do is to say the wrong thing every time," she concludes gloomily.

Or perhaps it is a teenager trying to impress another

person, or the high school crowd, only to fall flat on
his face instead. He looks himself over and is certain
that he's strictly no account, no poise, no looks, nothing
except a knack for doing the wrong thing. And the high
school girl is positive everyone noticed the old skirt her
mother made her wear, that she looked a fright anyway,
and when the folks won't cooperate with good clothes,
she has nothing to go on but her dreadfully plain face
and her hopelessly unglamorous hair.

We kick ourselves around quite a bit, don't we? If
other people talked half as nastily about us as we do of
ourselves, we'd really be upset.

But it's even worse when we come to real sins. We
may deny that we're doing wrong, but in our heart
we know it, and our heart condemns us bitterly and
savagely. We drag around with a feeling of guilt and
make ourselves miserable with remorse. A psychologist
has called the sense of guilt the most obvious fact
about man, and the most readily denied. Even people
who deny God and His law and go only by their own
standard know that they have fallen short of even their
own self-requirements. No man has ever been what he
wants to be. Thus, even when we lower the law to our
own human level, we fail it and are left with a sense
of failure and of guilt. And, having this guilt, we judge
ourselves harshly and make our lives miserable with self-
condemnation.

How are we going to get out of this pitfall of guilt
and condemnation that all men fall into? The answer is
a simple one: we can't get ourselves out. We always fail
even ourselves and, if we are honest, condemn ourselves,
and our situation is an inescapable one. Does this

> BECAUSE HE HAS FORGIVEN US, WE LEARN TO FORGIVE EVEN OURSELVES. THERE IS THEREFORE NOW NO CONDEMNATION EITHER FROM GOD OR FROM OUR OWN HEART.

mean that we remain trapped in condemnation, having trouble living with ourselves because we know our failure and our guilt?

Paul answered that for us when he wrote, "There is therefore now no condemnation to them which are in Christ Jesus" (Rom. 8:1). Christ as the perfect man took our condemnation on Himself and took its punishment also. He who was without sin became the guilty one in our place. As a result, when He becomes our life and lives in us, we have no condemnation. Instead, we have new life and peace in Him. Our sins are all forgiven and our guilt removed.

Paul told the Corinthians that he wasn't worried about their condemnation of him; in fact, he added, I don't judge myself, because I've already been judged and sentenced in Christ and am now forever free in Christ.

This gives us a new attitude towards ourselves, and we can now live with ourselves peacefully. Of course, we blunder; and of course, we sin. The old man in us makes this a constant fact of our existence. But now there's more to our lives than that. Jesus Christ is now part of our life, the overwhelming part of it, and no man can judge Him. Because He has forgiven us, we learn to forgive even ourselves. There is therefore now no condemnation either from God or from our own heart.

As a result, our life becomes very different. The old urgency and tension gives way to a peace and patience. We can say with David, "I will both lay me down in peace, and sleep: for thou, Lord, only makest me dwell in safety" (Ps. 4:8). "I laid me down and slept; I awaked; for the Lord sustained me (Ps. 3:5). "Thou has put gladness in my heart" (Ps. 4:7).

I shall this day and this week make my share of blunders and fall short, sinfully short, of the Lord's requirements of me. And yet I have this confidence, that He has already forgiven me and works in and through me in spite of myself. The old self-condemnation is gone, and in its place is peace and assurance: when I run, I shall not stumble, for the Lord is my confidence. For "in all these things we are more than conquerors through him that loved us" (Rom. 8:37; see also Ps. 4).

36

HOW TO LIVE WITH YOURSELF

PART 2 - ON GETTING THE MOST OUT OF LIFE

November 17, 1953

Good morning, friends. Last week we began a discussion of how to live with yourself. We saw that most people find it difficult to keep from judging themselves. We all fall short of God's law, but even the man who denies God's law can never avoid self-condemnation. He fails even his own self-made standard. No man has ever been what he wants to be. Thus, even when we lower the law to our own human level, we fail it and are left with a sense of failure and of guilt. And, having this guilt, we judge ourselves harshly and make our lives miserable with self-condemnation. We can only escape from this predicament as we accept Christ's sacrifice in our stead. He takes our condemnation, and we accept His new life and have freedom in Him.

This morning, let's look at another problem connected with living with ourselves. Many people are haunted by the fear that they are not getting the most out of life. This is true of teenagers, young married couples, the middle-aged, and the elderly: they feel that somehow they are missing something in life. Each one has his own reasons for feeling that way. One person feels that marriage is tying him down and keeping him from life. Some women feel that their children are stealing the best years of their lives and fret at missing out on so much freedom and fun. Others feel that lack of children is the reason why they are not really living, and they fret over this desert stretch in their lives. Then there are those who hate all morality and call it only prejudice: to them morals are merely chains keeping men from free life.

> NO MAN CAN GET THE MOST OUT OF LIFE UNLESS HE IS PREPARED TO GIVE THE MOST TO LIFE.

All around us people fret themselves sick over their failure to get the most out of life. They spend their years looking for life with growing unhappiness over their increasing inability to find it. There's nothing more pathetic than a dying man who fights against death because he feels that he hasn't had a chance to live yet. We can never live very peaceably with ourselves as long as we feel that our whole existence is made up of shadows rather than the real thing.

The fact that most people are not getting the most out of life and know they are not is a very encouraging fact. It tells us that God is still on His throne, and the penalty for neglect of Him and life apart from Him is a walking death. We act like living beings, but in our hearts we are dead to life and the world: everything has soured on us, and we find that nothing really pleases us any longer except our hopes and our imagination.

Our frustration is an encouraging fact because it demonstrates the relentless force of God's law. No man can get the most out of life unless he is prepared to give the most to life. And there most of us fail. We expect life to enrich us constantly but feel ourselves under no requirement to give ourselves to others in His name. Jesus said, "For whosoever will save his life shall lose it: but whosoever will lose his life for my sake, the same shall save it" (Luke 9:24).

This seems to put everything backwards. It says that the only way to get anything out of life is to expect nothing, and the only way to keep your life is to throw it away. Actually, this is the way things should be. The real trouble is not in life but in ourselves. As long as we make our wants and wishes central, we miss out on life, because life is never geared to us and our needs, but only to God and His requirements. If we take our new car, put it up on a foundation and try to live in it, we will miss the most of what that car offers us. That car was never invented to be anything but a motor vehicle: as such, it fits the bill. As a house, it's a miserable failure.

The same is true of our lives. We were made for a purpose, the service and the glory of the Lord. If we try to use our lives for any other purpose, we find ourselves frustrated by the obvious unfitness and unhappiness of our lives in anything but their godly function. And the Lord's purpose for us is simply this: our duty is not to get the most out of life but to give the most to it.

When we give, when we are ready to throw away our lives for His sake, then we get the most out of life. We see that our life here is a short span set against eternity. We see also that the only important thing in our lives should be to give ourselves as the Lord requires. Jesus said, "Seek ye first the kingdom of God, and his righteousness; and all these things shall be added unto you" (Matt. 6:33). We are not made to please ourselves but to please God. When we please Him, then we have peace and joy in Him and are able to live at peace with ourselves. As Andrew Murray stated it, "Do what God asks you to do: God will do more than you can ask Him to do." Give, and you shall receive. And the gift that He asks for is your life.

37

HOW TO LIVE WITH YOURSELF

PART 3 - NO PURPOSE

November 24, 1953

ood morning, friends. How to live with yourself has been our point of interest lately, and last week we took a look at people who are haunted by the fear that they are not getting the most out of life. We saw that no man can get the most out of life unless he is prepared to give the most to life. And there is where most of us fail. We expect life to enrich us constantly but feel ourselves under no requirement to give ourselves to others in His name. Jesus said, "For whosoever will save his life shall lose it; but whosoever will lose his life for my sake, the same shall save it" (Luke 9:24). As long as we make our wants and wishes central, we miss out on life, because life is never geared to us and our needs, but only to God and His requirements. We are not made to please ourselves but to please God, and in pleasing Him we get the most out of life.

This morning, let's take a look at another of the serious problems connected with living with ourselves. A great many people see no purpose to most things that happen to them. Life is a dreary journey through a desert of meaningless events with only here and there an oasis of meaning.

Many of us are inclined to feel that way. Troubles and sorrows often seem so senseless and pointless, that it almost seems wrong to try to read some meaning into them. But once we allow accident or chance to come into the world, we dethrone God and place most of our lives in the hands of chance rather than the Almighty. And the plain gist of all Scripture is that all things have their source and meaning in God.

LIVE FOR HIM, AND EVERY ACT, EVERY MOMENT, EVERY DUTY, EVERY TROUBLE AND SORROW HAS ITS ETERNAL MEANING IN HIM.

Let's face it this way then: you and I experience some things which are especially hard either to accept or to understand, and yet we have to take them as coming from the hand of God. How shall we read their meaning?

Moses gave us the clue when he wrote: "As an eagle stirreth up her nest, fluttereth over her young, spreadeth abroad her wings, taketh them, beareth them on her wings: So the Lord alone did lead him, and there was no strange god with him" (Deut. 32:11–12). Moses was writing about a certain kind of Palestinian eagle, one which nests high up on craggy cliffs. When the young ones are ready to fly, the mother stirs up the nest and kicks them out. The young ones begin to fall screaming towards the earth. The mother eagle then swoops under them, catches them, gives them a little time to catch

their breath and swallow their hearts, and then soars
high into the clouds. Then the frightened babies are
again dumped, and again fall screaming towards the
rocks below, only to be caught again by the mother's
strong back and wings. This process, a rough school of
life, continues until the young one suddenly understands
the mother's purpose and feels the power of flight in his
wings.

According to Moses, God treats us the same way. He
gives us no security in our tight little nest, but pushes
us into trouble that has us almost screaming in despair.
We feel like little eaglets, who perhaps wonder as they
fall why mama, so wonderful to them yesterday, has
suddenly become so vicious. They fail to see that they
were born for wings, and the only way to develop those
wings is to fall, and falling, learn to fly.

Some of us feel the same way about our Lord when
He lets us drop. We fail, like the eaglets, to see the true
purpose and meaning of life. We were born, not for this
world, but for eternity, and He lets us fall into trouble
that we might die more and more to this present life and
live increasingly to Him. The purpose is always there,
but we have to grow in Him to see it. But, if we live only
to ourselves, and only for this world, we live without
purpose, and our life becomes a sorry and a meaningless
thing.

Live for Him, and every act, every moment, every
duty, every trouble and sorrow has its eternal meaning in
Him. You have the confidence of a life that counts, and
all trouble that comes your way leaves you with those
eagle's wings a little better developed.

Are you falling through space these days? Are you

haunted with nightmares from nowhere which spell
a sickening and a meaningless life? Believe in this:
"The eternal God is thy refuge, and underneath are the
everlasting arms" (Deut. 33:27). You are not falling into
empty space and a meaningless death, but into the arms
of the eternal God. Surrender your life into His hands,
accept in faith His purpose and His love as revealed in
Jesus Christ, and you will find yourself, not falling onto
the jagged rocks, but soaring over the clouds and into
the sun.

38

HOW TO LIVE WITH YOURSELF

PART 4 - BEARING THE WORLD
ON YOUR SHOULDERS

December 1, 1953

ood morning, friends. In discussing the problem of how to live with yourself, we saw, last week, that a common failing of many people is the belief that there is no purpose to most things that happen to them. They believe that accident and chance rule most events and that God only acts occasionally. But Scripture asserts that God is active in every event, and not chance but purpose rules. Moses compared our life to that of young eaglets who are kicked out of their nest by the mother eagle. As they fall towards the earth, they scream in distress, apparently sure that there is neither purpose nor love in their mother's heart. They fail to see that they were born for wings, and the only way to develop those wings is to fall, and falling, learn to fly. The Lord treats us the same way when He lets us drop. We were born, not for this world, but for eternity, and He lets us fall into trouble that we might die more and more to this present life and live increasingly to Him.

This morning, let's take a look at another source

of trouble. A common sin is the attempt of many people to be another Atlas. Now Atlas, according to ancient Greek mythology, was a Titan who was punished by Zeus and compelled to carry forever on his back "the cruel strength of the crushing world." Thus Atlas stood forever in a place "wrapped in clouds and darkness," bearing the world on his shoulders.

> SOMEONE WHO IS FULLY CAPABLE ALREADY CARRIES THE WEIGHT OF THE WORLD, EVEN JESUS CHRIST, AND HE NEEDS NONE OF OUR HELP.

There are too many people nowadays who go around trying to carry the weight of the whole world on their shoulders. Life for them isn't complete without some worrying. They're always doing their share when it comes to the problems of communism: they carry it around like so much dead weight and worry about the world going up in atomic smoke, gas, or something worse. You're not a patriotic citizen, according to their estimation, if you're not half sick about something most of the time.

Is someone in the family sick or in trouble? Count on them to do their share by losing some sleep over it. They'll fret and stew about their friends and neighbors and hunt all over town for some new burden to carry as soon as an old one is lifted from their shoulders. Like Atlas, they feel that it's their duty to carry the world on their shoulders.

Are you trying to be a modern Atlas? If so, take another look in your mirror. You're a little too small and the world much too big, for the job to fit you. Besides, there is no vacancy for that job, so none of you need apply. Someone who is fully capable already carries the weight of the world, even Jesus Christ, and He needs none of our help. Instead, He offers to help us with our burdens, saying, "Come unto me, all ye that labour and are heavy laden, and I will give you rest" (Matt. 11:28).

You can live more easily with yourself if you realize that none of us are big enough to carry the weight of the world on our shoulders, or a burden for our friends. We're not able enough to carry our own burdens successfully. The only sensible thing to do is to turn them all over to the Lord in prayer, in this confidence, that He is able, and He doeth all things well.

Hallesby, in his fine little book, *God's Word for Today*, tells a pointed story concerning Old Mary, who was not very bright, and her neighbor. Old Mary used to walk into town for her groceries and then cart them home on her back. One day a neighbor rode up to the poor old woman and offered her a ride, which she gladly accepted. But instead of putting the heavy sack on the floor, she continued to shoulder it. When the bewildered neighbor asked her why she didn't put it down, Old Mary answered, "Oh, it's enough for you to give me a ride; the least I can do is carry the sack myself."

Foolish, of course. But aren't we all like that. The Lord takes us into His care, but we persist in hugging our burdens as though we were doing Him a favor and cooperating in His work! Old Mary was mentally retarded, and as long as we persist with our burden-carrying, we are spiritually retarded. We have a responsibility to carry them only as far as the place of prayer, and there to surrender them all to the Lord.

Remember, the Lord did pretty well with His creation before we came along, and He isn't in any trouble yet or likely to be. Remember also that you and I have messed up our lives whenever we have taken control, and whatever good there is in us is the Lord's mercy. It makes sense to stop trying to carry the world's burdens and ours, and to surrender them to the Lord. And since He has done so well with everything else, why not turn full control of our lives over to Him?

This is Scripture's counsel to us:

> In nothing be anxious; but in everything by prayer and supplication with thanksgiving let your requests be made know unto God." (Phil. 4:6, ASV).

> Casting all your care upon him, for he careth for you."(1 Pet. 5:7).

39

HOW TO LIVE WITH YOURSELF

PART 5 - BORROWED PROPERTY

December 8, 1953

Good morning, friends. We took a look last week at the people who try to be a modern Atlas, persons who try to carry the weight of the whole world on their shoulders. The foolishness of such burden-carrying is this: someone who is fully capable already carries the weight of the world, even Jesus Christ, and He needs none of our help. You and I mess up our lives whenever we take control, and whatever good there is in us is the Lord's mercy. It makes sense to stop trying to carry the world's burdens and ours, and to surrender them to the Lord. He has done so well with everything else, and can do the same for us when we give Him full control of our lives.

This morning, as we continue this discussion of how to live with ourselves, let's consider this matter of borrowed property. There have been a few occasions when I have found it necessary to drive a borrowed car. Once it was an old jalopy, another time a new car such as I never expect to own. In every case, I felt an extra responsibility in my driving. I took pains to be more

than careful, knowing that I had to return the car to its
rightful owner in good shape. It's the same way with
a borrowed house. We treat the dishes with extra care,
give the house a very careful cleaning, buy a present or
two, so that we can turn the place back to its owner with
thanks and in better than usual condition. If anything
goes wrong with the borrowed house, we feel fearfully
responsible. I remember that two years ago, when my
wife was staying in someone else's beautiful and newly
papered home, our little Sharon took a Crayola and went
all around the living room walls with it. There was some
hard work done, in the hour that remained before the
housewife returned home, to remove every trace of the
childish artwork!

Borrowed property involves a very real responsibility.
What belongs to someone else, we can treat only as
they please, or else we feel a guilty responsibility for
our waywardness. When we have mistreated someone's
property, we dread facing them with the sad news of our
neglect and irresponsibility.

And that's why most people are afraid to meet God.
They know they have mistreated His property. What is
God's property? Well, it's your life and mine, our bodies,
minds, and souls. He lent them to us. He's going to take
them back some day, and we know that we have abused
His property.

The tragedy of most men is that they try to steal
God's property and treat it as their own. The Greek
myth of Minos is a telling indictment of such attempts.
Poseidon gave Minos a gift which was to be returned
to him as a sacrifice, but Minos fell in love with it and
retained it. The result was the ruin of his home, the birth

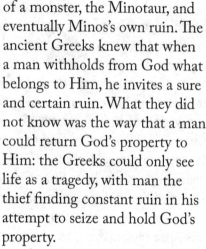

WE TREAT OUR LIVES WITH CARE AND RESPECT, KNOWING THAT THEY ARE NOT OUR OWN AND THAT WE ARE RESPONSIBLE FOR THEM.

of a monster, the Minotaur, and eventually Minos's own ruin. The ancient Greeks knew that when a man withholds from God what belongs to Him, he invites a sure and certain ruin. What they did not know was the way that a man could return God's property to Him: the Greeks could only see life as a tragedy, with man the thief finding constant ruin in his attempt to seize and hold God's property.

As Christians we recognize our basic depravity and selfishness. We realize that we have marred God's gift, our life, and that we have no natural desire to restore this property to its rightful owner. We also know that Jesus Christ does in us that which we cannot do of ourselves. We therefore ask Him to come in and do the house-cleaning so that when the Lord of the house returns, we can return Him His property in approved condition.

And day by day, we treat our lives with care and respect, knowing that they are not our own and that we are responsible for them.

Moreover, we know from our Lord's teaching that He expects a return on His investment. He gives us a talent and expects us return to Him five or ten in its place, declaring, "I reap where I sowed not, and gather where I did not scatter" (Matt. 25:26, ASV). He will not be satisfied with a mere return of what He has lent to us. It's easy to see from all this that the Lord demands a higher rate of interest than anyone else. As a result, we cannot treat His property and His investment casually and be able to live at peace with ourselves. Any man who abuses God's property and fails to return Him a good rate of interest on His investment is slated for trouble and distress.

Thus your life is God's property, and you owe Him a high rate of interest on it. You can live with yourself only if you have a clear conscience about this borrowed property, your life. Begin each day with God, by submitting your life into His hands and asking Him to live and work in you.

As John Calvin stated it: "It is the duty of believers 'to present their bodies a living sacrifice, holy, acceptable unto God'; this is the only true worship …We are not our own, therefore let us forget ourselves and our own interests as far as possible. But we are God's own, to him, therefore, let us live and die. We are God's own; therefore let his wisdom and will dominate all our actions. We are God's own; therefore let every part of our existence be directed towards him as our only legitimate goal."

40

HOW TO LIVE WITH YOURSELF

PART 6 - TALKING TOO MUCH

December 15, 1953

Good morning, friends. There's a particular sin, which most of us share, which gives us constant trouble but which we rarely try to correct. We have trouble trying to live peacefully with ourselves—or anyone else, for that matter—because of this sin, the sin of talking too much.

No doubt, there are some people who know enough to keep their mouths shut at the right time, but such people are usually pretty scarce. Calvin Coolidge was one of those men with a knack for silence. According to Mrs. Coolidge, her husband sometimes went for days without saying a word. Once when she asked him why he didn't speak to her, he remarked that he didn't have anything to say. I know an old Indian who operated on the same principle: he sometimes went for weeks without saying anything more than an occasional "good morning," and "good night." As a result, when he finally passed away, everybody had something nice to say about him, and nobody had a single criticism.

If people nowadays waited until they had something to say, there would probably be a deadly silence heard around the world. You'd be able to hear a pin drop in every government office in Washington. And you and I wouldn't have to kick ourselves so often for saying something we shouldn't have said.

WE LEARN SO MANY DIFFICULT THINGS. WHY CAN'T WE LEARN TO KEEP OUR MOUTHS SHUT?

Most of us *do* talk out of turn; we talk too much, and say too little of the right sort of thing. Why do we talk so much? What is it in us that drives us to say things over and over again that we have kicked ourselves for saying a dozen times in the past? We learn so many difficult things. Why can't we learn to keep our mouths shut?

We can understand our failure here if we look at the primitive meaning of speech. All over the face of the earth, we find that among primitive peoples language has a magical power. Among many tribes, for example, a dead person is never named, because to name him will bring back his spirit. For a person, especially a trained witchdoctor, to say certain evil things about a man means inevitable fulfillment: what has been said will happen. Their belief is that language or speech is power.

Now, obviously, this is primitive superstition, and we don't feel that it applies to us. But let's look at the reason behind this state of mind. The sin of man, according to Genesis 3, is that he tries to be a god and dethrones the true God from his own heart. And, in trying to be God, we imitate God. God's word is power, almighty and omnipotent power. "God said, Let there be light: and there was light" (Gen. 1:3). His word has creative power:

He speaks, and it is done. And man, in his pathetic and pitiful imitation of God, speaks in the vain belief that his word is power. We talk as though our saying will make things so. We criticize and judge as though we were Almighty God on His throne. We speak out insistently as though the world would stop in its tracks if we failed to get our little say-so in.

We talk too much, but the worst part of our talking is to God. Sometimes we talk and act as though the only real solution to all problems is for God to move over and let us run things for a while. We act as though His management has been a failure, and all that is needed is our own wise word to set things right. All this goes back to our fundamental sin, trying to be god. We don't keep our mouths shut because the old Adam in us keeps playing god and hoping that our saying will make things so.

We can be thankful for one thing: God has more patience with us than we have with Him, and so He puts up with us, and we can be grateful that He has a better sense of humor than we do, and so can laugh at the folly of man, playing god.

Then He speaks to us, in patience and wisdom, saying, "Be still, and know that I am God" (Ps. 46:10). Be still. Stop say-so. Stop trying to change things, and trust me to change them.

What we cannot do, He does. "And God said, Let there be light: and there was light." By His word He created the heavens and the earth, and His power is unchanged still. By His word, He has ordained and brought to pass all things, and His power is unchanged still. His arm has not grown short, nor has His sight grown dim. Be still, He says, and *know* that I am God.

When we stop talking so much, when we stop trying to be little gods, then we can in the silence of our heart, hear God. Then we understand the futility of our words, and we rely more and more on His Word. We are content to leave so much unsaid, because we know that the matter is in God's hands, not ours, and beyond the limits of His Word, we cannot speak. We live, then, in peace with ourselves, because we are at peace with our Lord; we know now that it is He who is God, and not we ourselves, and we are still and content, knowing that we are in the hands of an Almighty and omnipotent God who loves us and is able to deliver us. Be still this day, and know that He is God.

HOW TO LIVE WITH YOURSELF

PART 7 - LIVING IN A FAIRY-TALE WORLD

January 5, 1954

Good morning, friends. We're going to return today to our study of how to live with yourself. A sadly common failing of many people is this: they keep trying to live in a fairy-tale world. In fairy tales, the leading person, and that's always us, is pure and snow-white. The troubles are never due to the hero or heroine, but to a wicked king or stepmother. But, no matter what happens, in the end everything works out, and they live happily ever after. Nowadays, fairy tales are modernized and streamlined, but still much of what we get in movies, stories, novels, radio plays, and the like are really fairy tales. We hate to turn from them to the real world, where things simply don't happen that way.

We try to believe that our world is like the fairy tale and everything will work out to suit us, and we play along in that confidence. When I was a very small boy, I read a poem in a schoolbook which appealed to me enormously for that reason. I still like it. Remember Edward Lear's:

The Owl and the Pussy-cat went to sea
In a beautiful pea green boat
They took some honey, and plenty of money,
Wrapped in a five pound note

Life had no problems for them that would not
work out in a marvelous way. They sang by the light of
the moon and sailed away for a year and a day to find
rare and exotic fulfillment. Life was a breeze for them,
smooth sailing, and a song and a dance. That's what
makes it a fairy tale. You could change the characters
from the owl and the pussycat to Clark Gable and Rita
Hayworth, or any one of us, and it would still be very
much a fairy tale.

And this is the reason: In fairy tales, problems always
work out. In real life, problems are chronic. Instead
of working out, they move in to stay. In church work,
for example, the ministers who look for churches that
have no problems are usually the men who have the
worst problems to contend with. For in real life, it is
not problems that work out, but people. The problems
of today are not much different than those of Egypt,
Babylon, and Rome. Listen, for example, to these few
scraps of street conversation from the Roman Empire:
Listen to this war veteran gripe: "These wounds are the
return I get for trying to make democracy safe. Give
us some more help." And listen to this parent upset by
trends in education: "When the pupils graduate, they're
standing on their heads for all they know where they
are. And the reason why such blank idiots graduate from
our colleges is that life's only a set of lunatic syllogisms
to them." Or listen to a consumer complaining because
controlled food prices are favoring the producer only:

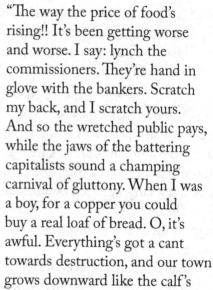

IN FAIRY TALES,
PROBLEMS
ALWAYS WORK
OUT. IN REAL
LIFE, PROBLEMS
ARE CHRONIC.
INSTEAD OF
WORKING OUT,
THEY MOVE IN
TO STAY.

"The way the price of food's rising!! It's been getting worse and worse. I say: lynch the commissioners. They're hand in glove with the bankers. Scratch my back, and I scratch yours. And so the wretched public pays, while the jaws of the battering capitalists sound a champing carnival of gluttony. When I was a boy, for a copper you could buy a real loaf of bread. O, it's awful. Everything's got a cant towards destruction, and our town grows downward like the calf's tail." That comment got an answer from a rag-and-bag merchant, who said, "Don't get so worked up about it. I hold there's nothing wrong with the country. It'd be a fine place if it wasn't for the people in it."

Sounds familiar, doesn't it? And yet all of that is Roman conversation—the same problems then as now. In real life, it is not problems that work out, but people. The fairy tale makes the world and its problems do the changing, while we remain unchanged, and it is this that marks the fairy tale approach. In actuality, the world changes very little, and its problems remain, and they are basically the same.

Thus you and I face a double demand on us. On the one side, the world says, you might as well give in, because I'm not doing the changing: you are. On the other side stands God Almighty, the unchanged and unchanging. It is you and I who must change. But in which direction?

Too many people, when they realize that their problems remain, and the world won't give, follow the path of least resistance: they give in to the world. Then their only hope in this frustrating defeat is to dream of a fairy-tale world, read fairy-tale books, and see fairy-tale movies. It is the consolation of the defeated to make these things their steady diet.

The path of victory is to give in, not to the world, but to the Lord. When a man or woman does that, then we can be confident of the outcome. Then, no matter what their problem or their situation, they have a power and a victory which overcomes the world. Don't look at the circumstances: they always spell defeat. Look at yourself, or the person you are concerned about: what are they showing signs of giving in to, the world or to God? If the surrender is to God, then remember this: there is nothing in this world that God cannot overcome, no matter what happens. He declares, "I am the Lord, I change not" (Mal. 3:6). And the psalmist observes,

> Of old hast thou laid the foundation of the earth: and the heavens are the work of thy hands. They shall perish, but thou shalt endure: yea, all of them shall wax old like a garment; as a vesture shalt thou change them, and they shall be changed: But thou art the same, and thy years shall have no end. (Ps. 102:25-27)

As John said:

> For whatsoever is born of God overcometh the world: and this is the victory that overcometh the world, even our faith. (1 John 5:4)

42

HOW TO LIVE WITH YOURSELF

PART 8 – MEANING AND PURPOSE

January 12, 1954

Good morning, friends. I hope that during these past two months or so that we have spent on how to live with yourself, one fact has been clear to all of us. You and I may have trouble living with our neighbors, our boss, our in-laws, our wife or husband, or anyone else, but none of these persons present us with half the problem that we are to ourselves. The hardest person to live with is ourself. If you can live with yourself, you can live with anyone.

Now, before we discuss this matter of how we can live with ourselves, I'd like to tell you about a book a friend gave to me about four or five years ago. This friend, having a keen interest in science, gave me Einstein's *Theory of Relativity*, saying that every intelligent man should read it. Well, I tried. Not very enthusiastically, but I tried. It didn't make much sense to me: the language was often meaningless to me, and the mathematical equations worse yet. So I quit. Because the book had no meaning for me, I couldn't take it.

Our lives are like that. If our life has purpose and

meaning, we enjoy and relish it. If purpose and meaning are lacking, we find it hard to live with ourselves. And I believe that's the reason for so much of our trouble today.

BOTH MEN AND WOMEN HAVE LOST PURPOSE AND MEANING, THE SENSE OF A CALL, FROM THEIR WORK, BECAUSE THEY THEMSELVES SEE NO PURPOSE IN LIFE ITSELF.

The great erosion of our time has been the erosion of purpose and meaning. Take the function and purpose of womanhood, for example. A modern psychiatrist, a woman at that, has remarked that for centuries the symbols of womanhood were the cradle, the distaff, and the spinning wheel, but now are the lipstick, handbag, and mirror, and the girdle. Substance has given away to appearance. Nowadays the census bureau, sociologists, and everyone in common regard a woman as "unemployed" if a housewife and mother. Yet a hundred years or so ago men would have said a woman was "unemployed" as a woman if not a housewife or mother. The home, in short, has lost its fullness of meaning, and many women find housework and motherhood as dull going as Einstein's book because the meaning is lost. The result is frustration and the feeling that the poor husband is a heel because he trapped her into marriage and its deadly routine.

The meaning is gone from men's work too. Men no longer speak of their occupation or trade as a calling. Instead, they'll tell you, "It's not a bad job; it's as good a racket as any." A racket is not a calling, and it has nothing to offer except money and tolerably pleasing working conditions.

Both men and women have lost purpose and meaning, the sense of a call, from their work, because they themselves see no purpose in life itself. As a result, it becomes a deadly and meaningless routine, and they find it hard to live with themselves.

We started with mathematics, so let's return to it for a moment. Supposing we take a million zeros and line them up—we have quite an imposing array of figures, but we still have exactly nothing. Add them up, multiply them, line them up, they still total nothing at all. But now take the number one and place it in front of them, and you have everything.

It's the same with our lives. The 365 days we shall live this year mean nothing in themselves. They can be a deadly and meaningless routine that gives us nothing but more bills, more gray hairs or perhaps just fewer hairs, and when we're through, none of those days add up to anything.

But the moment we take God and place Him first in our lives, at the beginning of everyday and foremost in every aspect, then the zero of our lives adds up to something by virtue of the power and meaning of God.

Then we can live with ourselves, because our lives have purpose and meaning. He gives us the life that knows not age, good things that do not pass away, and the delights that have no end. We can say with Simon Patrick of long ago, "Thy truth and faithfulness is my best security; Thy wisdom is my satisfaction in all events and accidents, Thy power is my support, protection and safeguard."

Jesus said, "Without me ye can do nothing," i.e., you are not able to do anything (John 15:5). In this impotence, we vex ourselves, become fretful at our meaningless life, and find it difficult to live with. In order to live with ourselves, we must first of all live with God as He is given to us in Jesus Christ. When we live with Him and in Him, we can repeat Isaiah's words,

Lord, thou wilt ordain peace for us: for thou also hast wrought all our works in us. (Isa. 26:12)

43

HOW TO LIVE WITH YOURSELF

PART 9 - GOD AND OTHERS

January 26, 1954

Good morning, friends. One of the facts I've been trying to illustrate these past few months is this, that the hardest person we have to live with is ourselves. No one gives us half the trouble we give ourselves.

Now, some people will dispute this fact. They insist that their lives would actually be very simple if all they had to do was to live with themselves. The trouble comes from their husbands, or wives, neighbors, friends, or bosses.

There's no denying, of course, that other people will give us considerable trouble at times in this world. Being a sinful world, it's never smooth sailing. We all have our share of headaches that somebody else thought up for us.

All this is true, and yet a person can live in very trying circumstances, put up with a completely worthless husband or a trying wife, and still live in peace and happiness if they have made their peace with God and are accordingly at peace with themselves. The world has countless people in it who live a happy life in unhappy circumstances. Those who feel that their life is being ruined by some man or woman, or certain trying circumstances, are usually their own worst troublemaker. Their constant complaint is that life is short-changing them, and that people have taken advantage of them. They enjoy brooding about their troubles and nurse a feeling of hostility and resentment towards the whole world, and especially towards those who do the

THE WORLD HAS COUNTLESS PEOPLE IN IT WHO LIVE A HAPPY LIFE IN UNHAPPY CIRCUMSTANCES.

most for them. They refuse to believe in goodness and suspect a dirty motive behind even the kindest act. They cannot believe in goodness, because they themselves are incapable of it, and they refuse to believe in anything better than themselves.

Such people cannot live with themselves any more than they can live with others. They would like to have you believe that their lives were peaceful before they met, married, or began working for so-and-so, but don't you believe it. Their whole life has been a volcano, and even when quiet on the surface, has been burning and boiling underneath.

The test of our lives, you see, is how we live with the Lord and with others. No man can live peacefully with himself who does not meet these two qualifications.

First of all, we must love the Lord with all our heart, mind, and being. This means relying not on ourselves but on Him, trusting not ourselves but the Lord. Now, when you love someone, you want to live with him, have all of his company you can get. If we love God, we enjoy His presence and companionship. We are then never alone, "for he hath said, I will never leave thee, nor forsake thee" (Heb. 13:5). Thus living with ourselves becomes a different proposition: it involves living with the Lord, and that takes away the staleness and dead bitterness out of our hearts and gives us a constant assurance and peace.

Second, we must love our neighbor as ourself. We are all of us good at talking peace, but very poor at living it. We believe that men and nations should get along peaceably, and then argue or fight about some little thing that doesn't matter. Our Lord said that the practical test of our faith is how we live with others. The Pharisees were precisely those who believed and did nothing, while the Good Samaritan was ready to help a man who belonged racially and religiously to a group that despised him. Only a man who lives with the Lord can consistently do that. He lives in peace and therefore carries peace. The troubles he has are not the important things in his life, but the Lord. He can say with David, "I will both lay me down in peace, and sleep: for thou, Lord, only makest me dwell in safety" (Ps. 4:8).

Old Thomas a Kempis said, "Set thyself first in peace, and then thou shalt be able to give peace to others." Don't blame others for ruining your life: probably you ruined it before you ever met them. If your inner life is a disturbed one, then you are the disturber of the peace, and no one else. A happy life is possible in unhappy circumstances if we live with the Lord, and if we are unhappy, it is usually likely that we have not made our peace with Him, or are unwilling to commit our live unreservedly into His hands, receiving all things as from Him.

You cannot live with yourself unless you can first live with the Lord, and then with others. Paul commanded us, saying:

If it be possible, as much as lieth in you, live peaceably with all men. (Rom. 12:18)

Owe no man any thing, but to love one another: for he that loveth another hath fulfilled the law. (Rom. 13:8)

HOW TO LIVE WITH YOURSELF

PART 10 - HANDS OFF!

February 3, 1954

G ood morning, friends. No doubt most of you have experienced something similar to my friend's experience who spent all of one winter scraping and soaking some paint off of a beautiful old table and chair set made of cherry wood. Finally, he had the ugly paint off and gave the chairs the coat of clear varnish that he felt would show off the beauty of the wood. But he had a messy job on his hands, because his wife, his two children, and every friend that came by touched the chairs to see if the fast-drying varnish had dried yet. With some people, a hands-off, do-not-touch, or wet-paint sign only invites meddling.

But before we feel too superior to such people, let's remember that most of us are natural-born meddlers. We may be very prim and proper about keeping our fingers off fresh paint or varnish, but how about the people's lives and private affairs we so cheerfully meddle with? Keeping our fingers off fresh paint doesn't make us virtuous—although it does keep our fingers clean!

The worst kind of meddling we do is with our own lives. We claim to be Christians, we say that we've surrendered our lives to the Lord, and yet we go on acting as though we were in control. We tell God our lives belong to Him, and then walk off with the keys, or else hug the steering wheel and ask Him to take the backseat. Is it any wonder that we have trouble living with ourselves? If we can't trust God with our lives, how can we dare trust ourselves? If we are dubious about leaving things in His hands, how can we ever hope to rest easy as long as they are in our hands?

Some years ago, a young freshman at Yale, class of 1909, decided to stop meddling with his life. He came from a famous family—anyone who reads ads knows the name, and he had all kinds of wealth—but William Whiting Borden realized that he himself could do nothing but mess up his life, and so young Borden, as a freshman, jotted down these words in his notebook:

Lord Jesus, I take hands off, as far as my life is concerned. I put Thee on the throne in my heart. Change, cleanse, use me as Thou shalt choose. I take the full power of Thy Holy Spirit. I thank Thee.

Young Borden died eight years later, a missionary in Egypt, a man whose life still carries an influence simply because Borden indeed had stopped meddling and had taken hands off his own life.

I know this is a hard thing to do. None of us have any right to complain about nagging, backseat drivers when we consider how we treat God. We feel it's all right for Him to take the wheel—as long as He does what *we* want Him to do. We go to Him with a list of things we want Him to do for us, and rarely do we ask what we can do in His service.

And yet when we become Christians the Lord hangs

> **WE GO TO HIM WITH A LIST OF THINGS WE WANT HIM TO DO FOR US, AND RARELY DO WE ASK WHAT WE CAN DO IN HIS SERVICE.**

a hands-off sign on our lives and asks us to leave everything to Him. We are assured that if we do as we are told, we "shall dwell safely, and shall be quiet from fear of evil" (Prov. 1:33). But we keep meddling as though God were incompetent. And that's a much worse thing than touching a little wet paint with the tips of our fingers!

Now, be honest with yourself: are you a meddler where your own life is concerned? Do you find it difficult really to trust God with yourself and your problems? If so, do you realize that what you are doing is placing your intelligence above God? And such an act is nothing but foolishness and sin.

A long time ago, David found that in time of trouble his only real consolation and hope was this: that his life was not in his hands, but the Lord's. His psalms are an expression of that faith. James Moffatt has given us a beautiful paraphrase of the first two verses of David's Psalm 62:

> Leave it all quietly to God, my soul, my rescue comes from him alone; rock, rescue, refuge, he is all to me, never shall I be overthrown. (Ps. 62:1–2)

Turn to Him this day, and lay all your burdens down before Him, "Casting all your care upon him; for he careth for you" (1 Pet. 5:7). He says unto us:

> Come unto me, all ye that labour and are heavy

laden, and I will give you rest. Take my yoke upon you, and learn of me; for I am meek and lowly in heart: and ye shall find rest unto your souls. (Matt. 11:28–29)

"BEYOND TODAY"

January 19, 1954

ood morning, friends. Sunday night, when I went home, I felt certain that nothing could keep me from going to bed and getting some much needed rest and sleep. I made the mistake, however, of picking up a small book, and, as a result, it was very much later, and only when the book had been read from cover to cover, that I got to bed.

I can't say that I enjoyed the book. Actually, it left me feeling more than a little ashamed of myself. The book is an autobiography, just recently translated from the Norwegian. Its author is Rolf Thomassen, the title, *Beyond Today*. Rolf Thomassen is a cripple, a spastic. Neither his feet, hands, nor his tongue are under his control. He cannot walk a step or bring a spoon to his mouth. His speech can be understood only with difficulty by strangers, and he spends his days in a specially designed chair, which is almost a trap, to hold him up and prevent him from falling out of it. Rolf Thomassen was born in October of 1902, and is now fifty-one years old. His life is and has been a hard one since the day he was born into a humble but gifted family, the twelfth of thirteen children. He entered life with only a helpless body, but his heart and faith have been strong. Rolf Thomassen learned to read, and then, by having a special collar strapped to his chin, with a small rod attached to the collar, learned to peck out words on a typewriter. His brilliant mind thirsted for self-expression, and, by holding a paintbrush between his teeth, he learned to paint, took lessons, and finally reached the point where he could support himself, and a maid to care for him, with the proceeds from the sale of his pictures. Musically inclined, he took a paintbrush, cut off the hairs, and used it to pluck at a zither, the brush held in his mouth, until he became a competent musician.

IF THE WORLD DISAPPOINTS US OR CRIPPLES US, OUR HOPE IS NOT ENDED. THE OUTCOME OF OUR LIVES IS NOT HERE BUT OVER THE LOFTY MOUNTAINS OF TIME AND IN ETERNITY.

Rolf Thomassen frankly admits that these accomplishments tend to leave him more frustrated. When he paints or plays, he is tormented by the thought of the music and the pictures he would like to express if only his body were not so limited. He is not happy about his affliction. In fact, he is clearly rebellious against it, hates it, and feels like a caged eagle. He is saddened by the knowledge that so much of life can never be his. And yet a friend of his can write, "It may sound like an exaggeration, but I believe I can truthfully say that Rolf Thomassen is one of the happiest persons I have met."

Rolf Thomassen himself says, concerning his affliction, that he feels the truth of the psalmist's statement, "by my God have I leaped over a wall" (Ps. 18:29): that he has clearly done. It would be a great day if each of us could surmount our barriers with as much faith and courage as this man. His parents could not give their afflicted son a sound body, but they did give him a sound faith, and the results have been great accordingly. To understand Rolf Thomassen's faith more clearly, let's look at the title of his autobiography: *Beyond Today*, in the English translation, *Over the Lofty Mountain*, in the Norwegian. As he himself says, on the last page of his book, "My future is light and long, it goes beyond the boundaries of time."

What makes his life more livable, gives him happiness in the midst of a hateful affliction, and confidence in the face of the long, hard years, is this: his life is beyond today, beyond this world, over the lofty mountains of time and into eternity. His life is hid with Christ in God.

We get so completely involved, sometimes, with the details of today, we identify our lives so intricately with the odds and ends of the daily grind that God finds it necessary to remind us through a man like Rolf Thomassen that our life is beyond today. If the world disappoints us or cripples us, our hope is not ended. The outcome of our lives is not here but over the lofty mountains of time and in eternity. The man to be truly pitied is not Rolf Thomassen but the man who lives only for today. It is he who loses his life and is left desolate and crippled in the end. Listen to these words of the man who lives beyond today, written after a hospital experience which failed to produce the greatly hoped for cure. He writes:

Why was I lying here grieving? What was I lacking? No, "the Lord is my Shepherd, I shall not want." What was everything in the world compared to the fact of being saved? Before I knew it, I was lying there jubilant, giving thanks for "the salvation, full and free," and the more I gave thanks, the more I was able to understand the depths of His finished work for me at Calvary…

I had to ask myself, "Why art thou so cast down, O my soul? And why art thou disquieted within me? Hope in God: for I shall yet praise him, who is the health of my countenance and my God."[1]

1. Rolf Thomassen, trans. by Torgrim and Linda Hannas, *Beyond Today* (Minneapolis, MN: Augsburg Publishing House, 1953), 89–90.

THE AUTHOR

Rousas John Rushdoony (1916-2001) was a well-known American scholar, writer, and author of over thirty books. He held B.A. and M.A. degrees from the University of California and received his theological training at the Pacific School of Religion. An ordained minister, he worked as a missionary among Paiute and Shoshone Indians as well as a pastor to two California churches. He founded the Chalcedon Foundation, an educational organization devoted to research, publishing, and cogent communication of a distinctively Christian scholarship to the world at large. His writing in the *Chalcedon Report* and his numerous books spawned a generation of believers active in reconstructing the world to the glory of Jesus Christ. Until his death, he resided in Vallecito, California, where he engaged in research, lecturing, and assisting others in developing programs to put the Christian Faith into action.

THE MINISTRY OF CHALCEDON

CHALCEDON (kal-SEE-don) is a Christian educational organization devoted exclusively to research, publishing, and cogent communication of a distinctively Christian scholarship to the world at large. It makes available a variety of services and programs, all geared to the needs of interested ministers, scholars, and laymen who understand the propositions that Jesus Christ speaks to the mind as well as the heart, and that His claims extend beyond the narrow confines of the various institutional churches. We exist in order to support the efforts of all orthodox denominations and churches. Chalcedon derives its name from the great ecclesiastical Council of Chalcedon (AD 451), which produced the crucial Christological definition: "Therefore, following the holy Fathers, we all with one accord teach men to acknowledge one and the same Son, our Lord Jesus Christ, at once complete in Godhead and complete in manhood, truly God and truly man...." This formula directly challenges every false claim of divinity by any human institution: state, church, cult, school, or human assembly. Christ alone is both God and man, the unique link between heaven and earth. All human power is therefore derivative: Christ alone can announce that, "All power is given unto me in heaven and in earth" (Matthew 28:18). Historically, the Chalcedonian creed is therefore the foundation of Western liberty, for it sets limits on all authoritarian human institutions by acknowledging the validity of the claims of the One who is the source of true human freedom (Galatians 5:1). The Chalcedon Foundation publishes books under its own name and that of Ross House Books. It produces a magazine, *Faith for All of Life*, and a newsletter, *The Chalcedon Report*, both bimonthly. All gifts to Chalcedon are tax deductible. For complimentary trial subscriptions, or information on other book titles, please contact:

Chalcedon • Box 158 • Vallecito, CA 95251 USA
www.chalcedon.edu

Get the First Volume of This Powerful Series, *Good Morning, Friends: A Collection of Weekly Radio Messages by R. J. Rushdoony*

From 1953 to 1956, Reverend R. J. Rushdoony gave weekly radio talks at Santa Cruz, California station KSCO that reveal a perfect blend of strong theology with poignant pastoral counsel. In fact, these insightful, concise messages are so well done they could be used for both individual and group discipleship at any level. They are a storehouse of wisdom, inspiration, strong doctrine, exhortation, and comfort for the Christian life.

Spanning subjects from the Reformed faith to the Trinity, life, suffering, prayer, the Bible, church, wisdom, and much more, you'll hear Rushdoony in a way you may not have heard him before. You'll sense he's speaking directly to you in pastoral fashion, and you'll enjoy every chapter.

CPSIA information can be obtained
at www.ICGtesting.com
Printed in the USA
FSOW03n1417240218
44788FS